# ELIZABETHAN PAGEANTRY

This painting of Queen Elizabeth is one of four bequeathed to the National Portrait Gallery by the late Harold Arthur Lee Dillon, 17th Viscount Dillon of Ditchley, Oxfordshire. It was painted to commemorate Queen Elizabeth's visit to Sir Henry Lee at Ditchley on 20th September, 1592. The artist is unknown.

# ELIZABETHAN PAGEANTRY

A pictorial survey of Costume and
its Commentators from c. 1560-1620

by H. K. MORSE

BENJAMIN BLOM    New York

BLK

# SPECIAL SPRING NUMBER
# OF THE STUDIO

First Published 1934
Reissued 1969 by
Benjamin Blom, Inc., Bronx, New York 10452

Library of Congress Catalog Card Number 68-56511

Printed in the United States of America

# CONTENTS

" Fashions then (in Adam's day) was counted a disease, and horses dyed of it ; But now (thankes to folly) it is held the onely rare phisicke, and the purest golden asses live upon it."    " *Guls Horne Booke* " *by Thomas Dekker.*

# FOREWORD

THE moralist and reformer which every age produces were not lacking in the sixteenth century. Here was superb cause for lamenting the extravagances of all classes, the lowly not excluded. Sumptuary laws restricting certain fashions according to the social and financial status of the wearer were made only to be broken, and humourless preachers published denunciations against excesses of all sorts, particularly that of dress.

Thomas Lodge writes in 1595 (*Wits Miserie*) :— " The farmer that was contented in times past with his Russet Frock and Mochado sleeves, now sels a cow against Easter to buy him silken geere for his credit."

From Philip Stubbes we have the following :—" And herby it appeareth that no People in the World is so curiouse in new fangles as they of England be . . . So that it is verie hard to knowe who is noble, who is worshipfull, who is a gentleman, who is not, for . . . those which are neither of the nobylitie, gentilitie, nor yeomanry . . . go dailie in silkes, velvets, satens, damasks, taffeties, and such like, notwithstanding that they be both base by byrthe, meane of estate and servyle of calling. This is a great confusion and a general disorder : God be mercyfull unto us."

We glean much from one Stephen Gosson, parson, who in 1595 wrote a series of verses entitled : *Pleasant Quippes for Upstart Newfangled Gentlewomen,* sub-titled : *A Glass to View the Pride of Fantastical Foreign Toyes Dailie Used in Womans Apparell.* The keynote lines run as follows :

" A patient heart cannot but rage
To see the shame of this our age."

I am attempting to show in the following pages the " spirit of the late Renaissance " from a costume viewpoint, allowing the occidentals of that amazing period to speak for themselves. Regional costume is for the most part not included in the scope of this work, which deals mainly with civilian attire, although things ecclesiastical, professional, ceremonial and military are included.

Assuming that the court was the fountain of fashion, we draw most of our pictorial information from that source. Thus are we supplied with first-hand evidence of what was actually worn by the so-called upper classes, or by those who could (or could not) afford indulgence in luxury. Notwithstanding Mr. Lodge's testimony, the poorer classes were of necessity slow to adopt the " new fangles."

With the exception of a few now rare contemporary works, there exists to my knowledge no monograph on costume of this great era. Although I lay no claim to fresh archæological discovery, I have endeavoured to compile this work on my gleanings from contemporary sources and from the combined opinion of the recognised authorities on the subject. I have gathered together from many sources both here and abroad more than eighty illustrations, many of which are familiar to you, and many I hope make here their first appearance as costume material.

I have pleasure in expressing my grateful appreciation of the courteous services at the New York Public Library, the Metropolitan Museum of Art, the Frick Art Reference Library of New York, the Library of Congress and the Folger Shakespeare Library in Washington. I wish also to acknowledge the helpful services rendered at the Victoria and Albert Museum, the British Museum, the Witt Library of Photographs, London, the Bibliothéque Nationale in Paris, and other institutions both public and private.

The hurried costume designer (he is usually hurried) will not labour through text—for him are the pictures. For the student of costume, I trust the glossary will prove useful. For all those laymen who love this flamboyant period for its own sake, I hope to rekindle an interest.

H. K. M.

Essex Fells, New Jersey.

October 1933.

# CONTEMPORARY DESCRIPTIONS
# OF MODES AND MANNERS

## HENTZNER DESCRIBES QUEEN ELIZABETH'S COURT

" . . . We were admitted, by an order Mr. Rogers procured from the lord chamberlain, into the presence chamber, hung with rich tapestry, and the floor, after the English fashion, strewed with hay, through which the Queen commonly passes in her way to chapel : at the door stood a gentleman dressed in velvet, with a gold chain, whose office was to introduce to the Queen any person of distinction that came to wait on her : it was Sunday, when there is usually the greatest attendance of nobility. In the same hall were the archbishop of Canterbury, the bishop of London, a great number of counsellors of state, officers of the crown, and gentlemen, who waited the Queen's coming out ; which she did from her own apartment when it was time to go to prayers, attended in the following manner : First went gentlemen, barons, earls, knights of the Garter, all richly dressed and bare-headed ; next came the chancellor, bearing the seals in a red-silk purse, between two : one of which carried the royal sceptre, the other the sword of state, in a red scabbard, studded with golden Fleurs de Lis, the point upwards : next came the Queen, in the sixty-fifth year of her age, as we were told, very majestic ; her face oblong, fair, but wrinkled ; her eyes small, yet black and pleasant ; her nose a little hooked ; her lips narrow, and her teeth black (a defect the English seem subject to, from their too great use of sugar) ; she had in her ears two pearls, with very rich drops ; she wore false hair, and that red ; upon her head she had a small crown . . . Her bosom was uncovered, as all the English ladies have it till they marry ; and she had on a necklace of exceeding fine jewels ; her hands were small, her fingers long, and her stature neither tall nor low ; her air was stately, her manner of speaking mild and obliging. That day she was dressed in white silk, bordered with pearls of the size of beans, and over it a mantle of black silk, shot with silver threads ; her train was very long, the end of it borne by a marchioness ; instead of a chain, she had an oblong collar of gold and jewels. As she went along in all this state and magnificence, she spoke very graciously, first to one, then to another, whether foreign ministers, or those who attended for different reasons, in English, French, and Italian ; . . . whoever speaks to her, it is kneeling ; now and then she raises some with her hand. While we were there, W. Slawata, a Bohemian baron, had letters to present to her ; and she, after pulling off her glove, gave him her right hand to kiss, sparkling with rings and jewels, a mark of particular favour ; wherever she turned her face, as she was going along, everybody fell down on their knees. The ladies of the court followed next to her, very handsome and well-shaped, and for the most part dressed in white ; she was guarded on each side by the gentlemen pensioners, fifty in number, with gilt battle-axes. In the anti-chapel next the hall, where we were, petitions were presented to her, and she received them most graciously, which occasioned the acclamation of ' Long Live Queen Elizabeth ! '   She answered it with, ' I thank you, my good people.' In the chapel was excellent music ; as soon as it and the service was over, which scarce exceeded half an hour, the Queen returned in the same state and order, and prepared to go to dinner.   But while she was still at prayers, we saw her table set out with the following solemnity : A gentleman entered the room bearing a rod, and along with him another who had a table cloth, which, after they had both kneeled three times with the utmost veneration, he spread upon the table, and after kneeling again, they both retired.   Then came two others, one with the rod again, the other with a salt-cellar, a plate and bread ;  when they had kneeled, as the others had done, and placed what was brought upon the table, they too retired with the same ceremonies performed by the first.   At last came an unmarried lady (we were told she was a countess) and along with her a married one, bearing a tasting-knife ;  the former was dressed in white silk, who when she had prostrated herself three times in the most graceful manner, approached the table, and rubbed the plates with bread and salt, with as much awe as if the Queen had been present :  when they had waited there a little while, the yeomen of the guard entered, bare-headed, cloathed in scarlet, with a golden rose upon their backs, bringing in at each turn a course of twenty-four dishes, served in plate most of it gilt ;  these dishes were received by a gentleman in the same order they were brought, and placed upon the table, while the lady-taster gave to each of the guards a mouthful to eat, at the particular dish he had brought, for fear of any poison.   During the time that this guard, which consists of the tallest and stoutest men that can be found in all England, being carefully selected for this service, were bringing dinner, twelve trumpets and two kettle-drums made the hall ring for half an hour together.   At the end of this ceremonial, a number of unmarried ladies appeared, who, with particular solemnity, lifted the meat off the table, and conveyed it into the Queen's inner and more private chamber, where, after she had chosen for herself, the rest goes to the ladies of the court.   The Queen dines and sups alone, with very few attendants ;  and it is very seldom that any body, foreigner or native, is admitted at that time, and then only at the intercession of somebody in power."

From *Hentzner's Travels*, 1598, as quoted by Nichols in his
*Progresses of Queen Elizabeth.*

## FASTIDIOUS BRISK AND THE DUEL

" He again lights me here—I had on a gold cable hatband, then new come up, which I wore about a murrey French hat I had—[he] cuts my hatband, and yet it was massy goldsmith's work—cuts my brims, which, by good fortune, being thick embroidered with gold twist and spangles, disappointed the force of the blow : nevertheless it grazed on my shoulder, takes me away six purls of an Italian cut-work band I wore, cost me three pound in the Exchange but three days before . . . He, making a reverse blow, falls upon my embossed girdle—I had thrown off the hangers a little before, . . . strikes off a skirt of a thick-laced satin doublet I had, lined with four taffatas, cuts off two panes embroidered with pearl, rends through the drawings-out of tissue, enters the linings, and skips the flesh . . . not having leisure to put off my silver spurs, one of the rowels catch'd hold of the ruffle of my boot, and, being Spanish leather, and subject to tear, overthrows me, rends me two pair of silk stockings, that I put on, being somewhat a raw morning, a peach colour and another, and strikes me some half inch deep into the side of the calf : he . . . takes horse, and away : I, having bound up my wound with a piece of my wrought shirt . . . rid after him, and, lighting at the court gate both together, embraced, and march'd hand in hand up into the presence.   Was not this business well carried ? "

Ben Jonson—*Every Man out of his Humour*, 1600.

## BUSINO GOES TO A THEATRE IN LONDON

Orazio Busino, chaplain to the Venetian Ambassador to James I, describes an incident during his visit to the Fortune Theatre, London.  1617 and 1618.

" ' . . . These theatres are frequented by a number of respectable and handsome ladies, who come freely and seat themselves among the men without the slightest hesitation.   On the evening in question his Excellency and the Secretary were pleased to play me a trick by placing me amongst a bevy of young women. Scarcely was I seated ere a very elegant dame, but in a mask, came and placed herself beside me . . . She asked me for my address both in French and English ; and, on my turning a deaf ear, she determined to honour me by showing me some fine diamonds on her fingers, repeatedly taking off no fewer than three gloves, which were worn one over the other . . . This lady's bodice was of yellow satin richly embroidered, her petticoat of gold tissue with stripes, her robe of red velvet with a raised pile, lined with yellow muslin with broad stripes of pure gold. She wore an apron of point lace of various patterns : her head-tire was highly perfumed, and the collar of white satin beneath the delicately-wrought ruff struck me as extremely pretty.' "

As quoted in Furnivall's edition of Harrison's *Description of England*

## SIR PHILIP SIDNEY AND THE TOURNAMENT

*The following is a contemporary description of the apparel of the challengers and their company preceding a notable tournament performed before Queen Elizabeth at Whitehall in the year* 1581.

*For the convenience of the reader it has been deemed wise to present such a lengthy passage in modern spelling.*

" First, the earle of Arundel entered the Tilt Yard, all in gilt and engraven armour, with caparisons and furniture richly and bravely embroidered, having attendant on him two gentlemen ushers, four pages riding on four spare horses, and twenty of his gentlemen.   All which aforesaid were apparelled in short cloaks and Venetian hose of crimson velvet, laid with gold lace, doublets of yellow satin, hats of crimson velvet with gold bands and yellow feathers, and yellow silk stocks.   Then had he six trumpeters that sounded before him ; and thirty-one yeomen that waited after him apparelled in cassock coats, and Venetian hose of crimson velvet, laid on with red silk and gold lace, doublets of yellow taffeta, hats of crimson taffeta, with yellow feathers, and yellow worsted stockings.

" After him proceeded the lord Windsor, in gilt and engraven armour, with caparisons and furniture, richly embroidered with gold, having attendant on him four pages riding on four spare horses, and four and twenty gentlemen, all apparelled in short cloaks of scarlet, lined through with orange tawny taffeta, and laid about with silver lace, doublets of orange tawny satin, Venetian hose of orange tawny velvet, black velvet caps, with silver bands and white feathers, and silver rapiers and daggers, with scabbards of black velvet ;  four trumpeters, and two footmen in cassock coats and Venetian hose of orange tawny velvet, and black velvet caps with silver bands and white feathers, four grooms of his stable leading of his four horses, in cassock coats and Venetian hose of orange tawny taffeta and orange tawny felts with silver bands and white feathers.   Then had he three score yeomen in coats of orange tawny cloth, with the unicorne of silver plate on their sleeves, and orange tawny felts with silver bands and white feathers.

" Then proceeded master Philip Sidney, in very sumptuous manner, with armour part blue, and the rest gilt and engraven, with four spare horses, having caparisons and furniture very rich and costly, as some of cloth of gold embroidered with pearl, and some embroidered with gold and silver feathers, very richly and cunningly wrought :  he had four pages that rode on his four spare horses, who had cassock coats, and Venetian hose of all cloth of silver, laid with gold lace, and hats of the same with gold bands and white feathers, and each one a pair of white buskins.   Then had he a thirty gentlemen and yeomen, and four trumpeters, who were all in cassock coats and Venetian hose of yellow velvet, laid with silver lace, yellow velvet caps with silver bands and white feathers, and every one a pair of white buskins ;  and they had upon their coats, a scroll or band of silver, which came scarfe-wise over the shoulder, and so down under the arm, with this poesie, or sentence, written upon it, both before and behind, *Sic nos non nobis*.

" Then came master Fulke Grevill, in gilt armour, with rich and fair caparisons and furniture, having four spare horses with four pages riding upon them, and four trumpeters sounding before him, and a twenty gentlemen and yeomen attending upon him, who, with the pages and trumpeters, were all apparelled in loose jerkins of tawny taffeta, cut and lined with yellow sarsenet, and laid with gold lace, and cut down the arm and set with loops and buttons of gold, Venetian hose of the same lined (as aforesaid) laid with gold lace down the side with loops and buttons of gold, with each a pair of yellow worsted stockings, and hats of tawny taffeta, with gold bands and yellow feathers."

From Holinshed's Chronicle as quoted by Nichols in his *Progresses of Queen Elizabeth*.

## ENTERTAINMENT AT THE COURT OF QUEEN ELIZABETH

" . . . Then a dance was begun. Men and women linked hands as in Germany. The men donned their hats or bonnets, although otherwise no one, however exalted his rank, may put on his hat in the Queen's chamber, whether she be present or not. The dancers danced behind one another as in Germany, and all the dancers, ladies and gentlemen, wore gloves. Though the dance at first sight seemed to be of German nature, it was no German dance, for they made a few steps forward and then back again. Finally they separated. The couples changed among one another but at the right moment each dancer returned to his or her partner. While dancing they very often courtesied to one another and every time the men bowed before their lady partners they doffed their hats. Slender and beautiful were the women who took part in this dance and magnificently robed. This dance was danced only by the most eminent who were no longer very young. But when it was over the young men laid aside their rapiers and cloaks, and clad in doublet and hose invited the ladies to dance. They danced the galliard and the Queen meanwhile conversed with those who had danced. The dancing over, the Queen waved her hand to those present and retired to her chamber . . . But as long as the dancing lasted, she summoned young and old and spoke continuously. All of them . . . knelt before her. She chatted and jested most amiably with them, and pointing with her finger at the face of one Master or Captain Rall [Herr von Klarwill believes this to be Raleigh], told him that there was smut on it. She also offered to wipe it off with her handkerchief, but he anticipating her removed it himself."

Von Wedel's account, 1585, in *Queen Elizabeth and Some Foreigners*,
edited by Victor von Klarwill.

## APPAREL OF THE GERMANS

" Their Earles (vulgarly called Graves) and their Knights, sometimes weare gold chaines, made of extraordinary great linkes, and not going more than once about the necke. . . Citizens Wives in some places weare upon their heads little caps in the form of an Oyster-shell, and they weare short cloakes, reaching no further then their elbowes.

"Upon the forepart of the head the Gentlewomen weare a border of pearle, and all others from the highest to the lowest, commonly weare garlands of roses (which they call Crantzes). Only women weare these Garlands in Winter, but in Summer time men of the better sort weare them within doores, and men of the common sort weare them going abroade . . . Many of the said Virgines have their neckbands set with spangles, such as some children with us weare. The Virgines in generall, weare linnen sleeves about their armes, as close as they can be made, for they esteeme it the greatest grace to have the smallest armes, and their petticoates are guarded with some ten or more fringes or laces of silke or velvet, each fringe being of a different colour one from the other, making the skirts thereof as variable in colour as the Raine-bow.

" Citizens wives put off their ruffes when they goe out of the house, covering their neckes and mouths with a linnen cloth for feare of cold.   And they weare great heavy purses by their sides, with great bunches of keyes hanging by chaines of brasse or silver :  and all generally, as well married women as Virgins, goe with bare legges . . . and the maide servants and married women of the inferiour sort weare no shoes except they goe out of the house, and a great part goe also abroade bare footed.   The married women hide their naked feete with long gownes, but the maide servants wearing short gownes, and girding them up with a roule some handfull under the wast about their hippes (especially in the lower parts of Germany) many times offend chast eyes with shewing their nakednesse, especially when they stoope for anything to the ground.   And in those parts of Germany the Citizens wives, like our little children, weare red and yellow shooes, and guilded at the toes.

"In general it is disgracefull to married women or Virgines (excepting in Ausburg, and some few other cities) to goe out of doores without a cloake, which commonly is of some light stuffe, as Grogram, or the like, faced with some furres, and at Hidelberg they never goe abroade without a little basket in their hands, as if they went to buy something . . .

" In many places the ordinary citizens Wives have their gownes made with long traines, which are pinned up in the house, and borne up by maide servants when they goe abroade, which fashion of old onely great Noblemen used with us.   And in many cities as well the married as unmarried Women weare long fardingales, hanging about their feete like hoopes, which our Women used of olde, but have now changed to short fardingales about their hippes."

Moryson—Itinerary, 1605-17.

## MORYSON DISCUSSES THE BOHEMIANS

" The Bohemians are apparelled much like the Germans, and delight in greene, yellow, and light colours, but more frequently weare silkes and velvets than the Germans, and also false jewels of their owne.   And many times they weare blacke cloth with many laces or fringes of light colours, each fringe differing in colour one from the other.

" The married Gentlewomen attire their heads like our Virgins, and in like sort beare up their haire on the forehead with a wier.  They use with the Germans to make their gownes with traines, or to beare them out with long fardingals, and to weare short cloakes.

" Citizens wives weare upon their heads large gray caps, rugged like gray Connie skinnes, and formed like the hives of Bees, or little caps of velvet close to the head, of a dunne colour, with the hinder skirt (or hinder part) cut off and open.   And upon their legges they weare white buskins, wrought with velvet at the toes ; but upon their armes they weare large sleeves and, contrary to the Germans, thinke them to be most comely."

Moryson—Itinerary.

## NETHERLANDISH ATTIRE

" In the united Provinces, the Inhabitants, being for the most part Merchants and Citizens, the Men use modest attire of grave colours, and little beautified with lace or other ornament . . .

" . . . For as well men as women for their bodies and for all uses of the Family, use very fine linnen ; and I think that no clownes in the World weare such fine shirts as they in Holland doe.

" Some of the chiefe Women not able to abide the extreme cold, and loth to put fier under them for heate (as the common use is) because it causeth wrinckles and spots on their bodies, doe use to weare breeches of linnen or silke.

" All Women in generall when they go out of the house, put on a hoyke or vaile which covers their heads, and hangs downe upon their backs to their legges ; and this vaile in Holland is of a light stuffe or Kersie, and hath a kinde of horne rising over the forehead, not much unlike the old pummels of our Womens saddles, and they gather the Vaile with their hands to cover all their faces, but onely the eyes."

Moryson—*Itinerary.*

## THE SWEITZERS

" The Sweitzers, being Citizens (for their nobility is long since rooted out by popular seditions) weare large round caps (such as are used by our Prentices and Students in the Innes of Court), and together with them they weare cloakes (whereas with us they are onely used with gownes), yea, and Swords also (which seemed strange to be worne with caps).   They weare great large puffed breeches, gathered close above the knees, and each puffe made of a diverse light colour ; but their doublets are made close to the body.   The married Women cover their heads with a linnen coyfe, and upon it weare such caps as the men use (which are broader than we use in England) and commonly weare a linnen crossecloth upon the forehead. To be briefe, the Virgins goe bare headed with their haire woven up, and use short cloakes, and as well married as unmarried Women, as also the Men, are apparelled like the Germans, and affect nothing lesse then pride in their attire."

Moryson—*Itinerary.*

## THE SWISS GUARDS AT THE COURT OF FRANCE

" Switzers weare no coates, but doublets and hose of panes intermingled with red and yellow and some with blew trimmed with long puffes of yellow and blew sarcanet rising up betwixt the panes, besides codpieces of the like colours . . . I observed that all these Switzers do weare velvet cappes with feathers in them and I noted many of them to be very clusterfisted lubbers.   As for their attire, it is made so phantastically that a novice newly come to Court, who never saw any of them before, would halfe imagine, if hee should see one of them alone without his weapon, he were the Kings foole."

*Coryat's Crudities,* 1611.

## MORYSON ON FRENCH ATTIRE

" . . . Gentlemen weare mixed light colours, and silk garments, laid with silke lace, and sattens, commonly raced, and stockings of silke or of some light stuffe, but never woolen or worsted (which only Merchants weare) and imbrodered garments, with great inconstancy in the fashion, and negligently or carelessly, which the Germans call slovenly, because they many times goe without hat bands and garters, with their points untrust, and their doublets unbutoned . . .

" In generall men and women (excepting Courtiers and some of the Gentry) weare light stuffes, and rather delicate then sumptuous garments . . . Merchants weare blacke garments of cloth, or light stuffes of silke, commonly after a modest fashion.

" The Senators weare cloakes and hats (not gownes and caps as ours use) and onely the Presidents and Counsellers of Parliaments weare scarlet gownes, and that onely at solemne times, as the first day that the Court sits, and all the Procurators daily weare gownes.

" In generall the women married cover their heads with a coyfe or netted cawle. The Gentlewomen beare up their haire on the fore-heades with a wier, and upon the back part of the head weare a cap of other haire then their owne, over their cawle, and above that they weare a coyfe of silke, lined with Velvet, and having a peake downe the forehead. Or else the gentlewomen and wives of rich Merchants with small difference of degree, weare upon their heads a blacke vail of Cipers, peaked at the forehead, with a velvet hood hanging downe behind ; onely the Gentlewomen weare this hood gathered, and the Merchants wives plaine.

" Both men and women lately used falling bands, which the better sort starched, and raised up with wier, shewing their necks and breasts naked. But now both more commonly and especially in winter, weare thicke ruffes.

" Gentlewomen and citizens wives when they go out of dores, weare upon their faces little Maskes of silk, lined with fine leather, which they alwaies unpin, and shew their face, to any that salutes them. And they use a strange badge of pride, to weare little looking glasses at their girdles.

" In France as well men as women, use richly to be adorned with Jewels. The men weare rings of Diamonds, and abroad Jewels in their hats, placed upon the roote of their feathers. The Ladies wear their Jewels commonly at the brest, or upon the left arme, and many other waies ; for who can containe the mutable French in one and the same fashion ? "

Moryson—Itinerary

## ITALIAN APPAREL AS DESCRIBED BY MORYSON

" Of the Italians it is proverbially said, that the Venetians are gowned, yet by night going to visit their Mistresses, weare short Spanish cloakes.—That those of Ferrara and Mantua are proud of their attire, with their caps set with gold buttons. That the Florentines are ridiculous (yet I observed none more modestly attired). That those of Genoa are neate and comely in attire, but weare no gownes, nor lace, nor gardes.   That those of Milan are decent, and the Neapolitans are glittering and sumptuous.

" When they take journeyes, they weare large bootes, that they may fling off being untied, but such as keepe them dry in all weathers ; and to the same ende they weare thicke felt hats and short felt clokes, which no rain can pierce . . .

" And howsoever their apparrell is soft and delicate, yet they onely weare cloth and stuffes made at home, not any brought from forraigne parts.

" And howsoever all those mixed colours which we so highly esteeme, come from thence, yet are they not invented by the Italians, but by the Factors of our Merchants, who lie there of purpose, to feede the fantasticall pride of our Youth, in new Stuffes, or at least new coloures and names.

" And the Senators, Doctors and Knights weare Scarlet gownes with large sleeves lined in winter with rich furres . . . And the Gentlemen constantly weare these gownes, either in singular pride to be knowne from others (for no Citizens, nor any Gentlemen of other Cities weare gownes) or for obedience to the Law, or out of an old custome, which the most wise Magistrates permit not to be broken.   And for the same cause, all the gentlemen, none excepted, weare little caps of Fleese or Cloth hardly covering the crowne, or the forepart of the head." [Coryat in a similar description adds their " flappes of crimson velvet cast over their left shoulder."]

" Lastly, in great wisdome they care not to have rich apparrell, but hold it honourable to live of their owne.   They make no fine linnen, and therefore use course linnen, both for shirts, and other uses of the Family, and commonly weare little falling bands, and many times ruffes of Flanders linnen, sometimes wrought with Italian Cut-worke, much used with us, but their ruffes are not so great as ours, and they have little skill in washing, starching and smoothing linnen.

" They weare very short haire, as all Nations doe that live in hot climes, the contrary vice of wearing longe haire being proper to the French, English, and Scots, but especially the Irish . . .

" Among the Princes of Italy, I did see Ferdinand the third, Duke of Florence, who did weare a cloke of English cloth, with one little lace, and breeches of Velvet without any ornament, and stockings of leather and a leather scabbard to his sword, and his coach was lined with old greene Velvet, and the horses seemed taken out of the plough.

" The women of Venice weare gownes, leaving all the necke and brest bare, and they are closed before with a lace, so open, as a man may see the linnen which they lap about their bodies, to make them seeme fat, and Italians most loving fat women. They shew their naked necks and breasts, and likewise their dugges, bound up and swelling with linnen, and all made white by art.

" They weare large falling bands, and their haire is commonly yellow, made so by the Sunne and art, and they raise up their haire on the forehead in two knotted hornes, and deck their heads and uncovered haire with flowers of silke and with pearle, in great part counterfeit.   And they cast a black vaile from the head to the shoulders, through which the nakednesse of their shoulders, and neckes, and breasts, may easily be seene.   For this attire the women of Venice are proverbially said to be Grande di legni, Grosse di straci, rosse di bettito, bianche di calcina: that is tall with wood, fat with ragges, red with painting, and white with chalke.

" In generall the Women of Italy . . . most commonly (but especially the wives of shopkeepers) weare gowns of silke and light stuffes, yea woven with gold, and those close at the brest and necke, with a standing collar, and little ruffes close up to the very chinne, and shewing no part naked.

" The city Virgins, and especially Gentlewomen, cover their heads, face and backes with a Vaile, that they may not be seene passing the streetes, and in many places weare silke or linnen breeches under their gownes.  Also I have seene honorable Women, as well married as Virgines, ride by the high way in Princes traines, apparelled like Men, in a doublet close to the body, and large breeches open at the knees, after the Spanish fashion, both of carnation silke or sattin, and likewise riding astride like men upon Horses or Mules, but their heads were attired like Women, with bare haires knotted, or else covered with gold netted cawles, and a hat with a feather.

" And many times in the Cities (as at Padua) I have seene Curtizans (in plaine English, whores) in the time of shroving, apparrelled like men, in carnation and light coloured doublets and breeches, and so playing with rackets at Tennis with yong men, at which time of shroving, the Women no lesse then Men (and that honourable women in honourable company) goe masked and apparrelled like men all the afternoone about the streetes, even from Christmasse holydaies to the first day of Lent.   The Women wearing Mens breeches have them open all before, and most part behind, onely buttoned with gold and silver buttons : and the Curtizans make all the forepart of their gownes in like manner open, to avoide wrinckling."

Moryson—Itinerary.

NOTE—Vecellio says, " in place of pearls, the prostitutes wear certain beads resembling pearls, and as pearls are forbidden them, one can guess their position when they uncover their throat . . ."   The above remark accompanies an illustration of a prostitute dressed modestly in black with a veil over her head, which she raises with one hand, thus revealing her face and neck.

Vecellio—Degli Abiti Antichi e Moderni, 1590.

## CORYAT GOES TO THE THEATRE IN VENICE

" I was at one of their Play-houses, where I saw a Comedie acted.   The house is very beggarly and base in comparison of our stately Play-houses in England : neyther can their Actors compare with us for apparell, shewes, and musick. Here I observed certaine things that I never saw before.   For I saw women acte, a thing that I never saw before, though I have heard that it hath beene sometimes used in London ; and they performed it with as good a grace, action, gesture, and whatsoever convenient for a Player, as ever I saw any masculine Actor.   Also their noble and favourite Cortezans came to this comedy, but so disguised, that a man cannot perceive them.   For they wore double maskes upon their faces, to the

18

end they might not be seene ; one reaching from the toppe of their forehead to their chinne, and under their necke ; another with twiskes of downy or woolly stuffe covering their noses. And as for their neckes round about, they were so covered and wrapped with cobweb lawne and other things, that no part of their skin could be discerned. Upon their heads they wore little blacke felt caps very like to those of the Clarissimoes that I will hereafter speake of. Also each of them wore a black short Taffata cloake. They were so graced, that they sate on high alone by themselves, in the best roome of all the Play-house. If any man should be so resolute to unmaske one of them but in merriment onely to see their faces, it is said that—were he never so noble or worthy a personage—he should be cut in pieces before he should come forth of the roome, especially if he were a stranger. I saw some men also in the Play-house, disguised in the same manner with double visards, those were said to be the favourites of the same Courtezans : they sit not here in galleries as we do in London. For there is but one or two little galleries in the house, wherein the Courtezans only sit. But all the men doe sit beneath in the yard or court, every man upon his severall stoole, for which he payeth a gazet."

*Crudities*, 1611

## VILLAMONT DESCRIBES THE VENETIAN LADIES

" Regarding the apparel of the Venetian married ladies, it is rather pretty, and their gowns are busked in front and back. They have their blond hair for the most part hanging nicely and arranged at the forehead in the shape of two horns half a foot high, without any iron mounting or other thing to hold them up, unless it were the charming braiding which they do themselves. They wear nothing on their head but a veil of black crepe which falls much below their shoulders, which does not prevent one from seeing the beauty of their hair, their shoulders and breasts which they show almost to the stomach. They appear a foot taller than the men, because they are mounted upon patens of wood covered with leather, which are at least a foot high, so that they are obliged to have a woman to aid them to walk, and another to carry their train, and walking with gravity go along showing their breasts, the old as well as the young. But the Romans, Milanese, Neapolitans, Florentines, Farrarans and other ladies of Italy are much more modest, for their patens are not so high, and also they do not bear their breasts.

" As to the widows, they are always veiled and covered until they remarry, and the girls never leave the house of their father after the age of fourteen until they are married, excepting Easter day when they go to mass and receive the body of Jesus Christ."

*Les Voyages du Seigneur de Villamont*, 1607

## CORYAT DESCRIBES THE JEWS IN VENICE

" I was at the place where the whole fraternity of the Jews dwelleth together, which is called the Ghetto, being an Iland : for it is inclosed round about with water. It is thought there are of them in all betwixt five and six thousand. They are distinguished and discerned from the Christians by their habites on their heads ; for some of them doe weare hats and those redde, only those Jewes that are borne in the Westerne parts of the world, as in Italy, &c. but the easterne Jewes being otherwise called the Levantine Jewes, which are borne in Jerusalem, Alexandria, Constantinople, &c. weare Turbents upon their heads as the Turkes do : but the difference is this : the Turkes weare white, the Jewes yellow. By that word Turbent I understand a rowle of fine linnen wrapped together upon their heads, which serveth them instead of hats, whereof many have bin often worne by the Turkes in London . . ."

Crudities

## CORYAT TELLS MORE ABOUT THE JEWS

" I saw many Jewish women, whereof some were as beautiful as ever I saw, and so gorgeous in their apparel, jewels, chaines of gold, and rings adorned with precious stones, that some of our English Countesses do scarce exceede them, having marvailous long traines like Princesses that are borne up by waiting women serving for the same purpose."

" Every one of them (Jews in the Synagogue at Venice) . . . weareth a kind of light yellowish vaile made of Linsie Woolsie (as I take it) over his shoulders, something worse that our courser Holland, which reacheth a little beneath the middle of their backes."

Crudities

## HE DESCRIBES AN ITALIAN FAN.

" These fannes both men and women of the country doe carry to coole themselves withall in the time of heate, by the often fanning of their faces. Most of them are very elegant and pretty things. For whereas the fanne consisteth of a painted peece of paper and a wooden handle ; the paper which is fastened into the top is on both sides most curiously adorned with excellent pictures, either of amorous things tending to dalliance, having some witty Italian verses or fine emblemes written under them ; or of some notable Italian City with a briefe description thereof added thereunto."

Crudities

## HE SEES IN ITALY AN UMBRELLA FOR THE FIRST TIME

" . . . many of them doe carry other fine things (than fans) of a far greater price, that will cost, at the least, a duckat, which they commonly call in the Italian tongue umbrellaes, that is, things that minister shadow unto them for shelter against the scorching heate of the sunne. These are made of leather, something answerable to the forme of a little cannopy, and hooped in the inside with divers little wooden hoopes that extend the umbrella in a pretty large compasse. They are used especially by horsemen, who carry them in their hands when they ride, fastning the end of the handle upon one of their thighes, and they impart so large a shadow unto them, that it keepeth the heate of the sunne from the upper parts of their bodies."

Crudities

*By* FRANÇOIS CLOUET                    *Vienna Museum*

" I cannot abide these round breeches, I am ready to swoon at them."

" *A Woman is a Weathercocke*," by Nathaniel Fielde

*Note long-skirted jerkin characteristic
of the early Elizabethan period.*

# LUCIA von MUNCHAUSEN

*By* LUDGER TOM RING *the younger*

" These apornes white of finest thred     So quaintlie cut, so richlie wrought,
So choicelie tide, so dearlie bought,     Were they in worke to save their cotes,
So finely fringed, so nicelie spred,     They need not cost so many grotes."

" *Pleasant quippes for upstart newfangled gentlewomen,*" *by Stephen Gosson*

*Note shoulder cape ; guards on kirtle ; head garland or " crantz."*

*Attributed to* ANTONIO MORO                    *Courtesy of the Hispanic Society of America*

Among the gifts received by Queen Elizabeth at "Newyers-
tyde" in the year 1585 is listed the following from the Earl
of Leicester : " First, a sable skynne, the hedd and four feete
of gold, fully garnished with dyamonds and rubyes of sundry
sorts."           *" Progresses of Queen Elizabeth," by John Nichols.*

*Note pomander.*

BIANCA CAPPELLO (*circa* 1560)

*By* BRONZINO

" . . . for fashion we are much inferiour to them [the Italians]."

" *Coryat's Crudities* "

## LADY OF THE VAVASOUR FAMILY

" The women also have dublets . . . buttoned up the brest,
and made with wings, welts, and pinions on the shoulder
points, as mens apparel is for all the world . . ."

*" Anatomy of Abuses," by Philip Stubbes*

*By* BARTEL BRUYN *the younger*          *Courtesy of M. Knoedler & Co.*

25

*By* FRANS POURBUS *the Elder*

[In a barber's shop] " . . . when you come to be trimed they will aske you whether you will be cut to looke terrible to your eniemie or amiable to your freend, grim and sterne in countenance, or pleasant and demure (for they have divers kinds of cuts for all these purposes, or else they lie).  Then when they have done al these feats, it is a world to consider, how their mowchatowes must be preserved and laid out, from one cheke to another, yea, almost from one eare to another and turned up like two hornes toward the forehead."

" *Anatomy of Abuses*," *by Philip Stubbes*

*Note pinking and razing.*

*By* LUCAS CRANACH *the younger*                                    *Vienna*

" A little Apish Hatte, cowched fast to the pate, like an oyster."
" *Welshman,*" *by Andrew Boorde*

*Note chains ; rings ; caul.*

*Painting in the Museum at Bayeux, attributed to* FRANS POURBUS *the elder*

*Courtesy of Archives Photographiques, Paris*

*Description of the painting.* Extreme left, Pourbus the painter. In light attire, Charles IX. With hand on breast, Henri Duc de Guise. Towards centre, Catherine de Medici, Queen Mother. Holding hand of Catherine, Duc d'Alençon. Background, wearing light turban, Duc d'Anjou, later Henri III. Extreme right background, Marie Touchet, mistress of Charles IX. Kneeling, Marguerite de Valois. Of the troupe are represented Brigella, Zanni, Pantaloon, Harlequin. (Minor parts are played by courtiers and ladies.)

" This painting stands as the oldest and most important document in the iconography of the Commedia dell'Arte now extant. [It] . . . probably represents the company of Alberto Ganessa giving a performance in collaboration with various personages at the Court of Charles IX."

" *The Italian Comedy,*" *by Pierre Louis Duchartre*

*See page* 114 *under Harlequinade.*

*Attributed to* FRANÇOIS CLOUET                    *Private Collection*

" In France as well men as women use richly to be adorned with jewels."

*" Itinerary " of Fynes Moryson*

## SIR CHRISTOPHER HATTON (*circa* 1575)

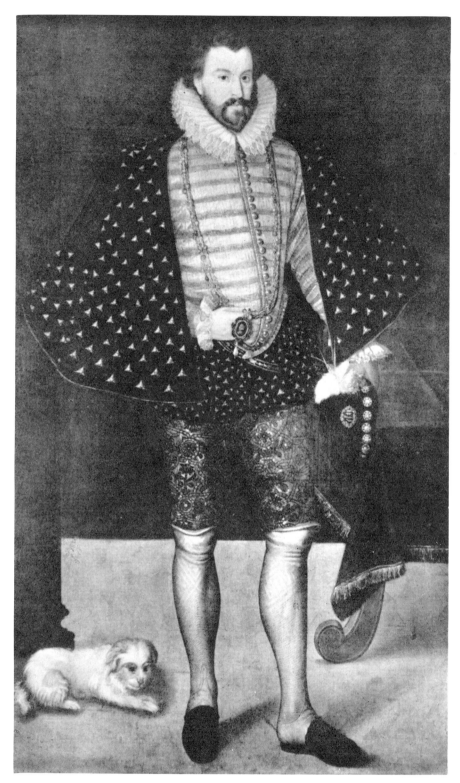

*By* CORNELIS KETEL          *Collection of the Earl of Winchelsea and Nottingham*

" . . . The day hath bene when one might have bought him two clokes for lesse than now he can have one of these clokes made, they have such store of work-manship bestowed uppon them."          "*Anatomy of Abuses*," *by Philip Stubbes*

*Note pantofles ; canions.*

*By* GIAMBATTISTA MORONI

*Courtesy of the Isabella Stewart
Gardner Museum, Boston, U.S.A.*

" Their garments are commonly of silke but seldome embrodred, and never laid with gold or silver lace, and commonly of black colour."

*" Itinerary " of Fynes Moryson*

31

*Enamel by* LEONARD LIMOSIN                    *Musée du Louvre*

"Another sorte of dissolute minions and wanton Sempronians (for I can term them no better) are so far bewitched, as they are not ashamed to makes holes in their ears whereat they hang rings and other Jewels of gold and precious stones. But what this signifieth in them I will hold my peace, for the thing it selfe speaketh sufficiently . . . But because this is not so muche frequented amongst Women as Men, I will say noe more thereof."
                    "*Anatomy of Abuses,*" *by Philip Stubbes*

". . . Our French women have lately taken up to pick and snip out the haires of their forehead."                    *Montaigne's Essays, tr. Florio*

*Anonymous*                                                                 *National Portrait Gallery*

" The collar . . . rose up so high and sharp as if it would have cut his throat by daylight." " *The ant and the nightingale," by Thomas Middleton*

*From " Habitus Varriarum Gentium,"* 1581, *by* ABRAHAM DE BRUYN

" . . . a German from the waist downward, all slops . . . Unless
he have a fancy to this foolery, as it appears he hath, he is no
fool for fancy, as you would have it appear he is."

Shakespeare, " *Much Ado About Nothing,*" *III, ii,* 35

RVSTICA MVLIER GALLICA.

CVI.
Ein Beurin in Franckreich.

RVSTICVS IN GALLIA.

CV.
Ein Frantzösischer Baucr.

*From " Habitus Praecipuorum,"* 1577, *by* JOST AMMAN

" . . . Women of the inferiour sort wearing . . . short gowns and girding them up with a roule some handfull under the waist about their hippes."

*" Itinerary "* of Fynes Moryson

## SAILORS FROM THE LOW COUNTRIES

Nauicularius Hollandus. Nauta Hollandus. Nauta habitus in ea parte Hollandiæ quam Aquaticam nominant. Communis fere nautarum amictus apud Belgas. Nauicularius Britannus. quem Britonem vulgo nominat

*From " Habitus Varriarum Gentium,"* 1581, *by Abraham de Bruyn*

*Anonymous*                                    *Detail from a painting in the Musée de Versailles*

" These flaming heads with staring haire,
        these wyers turnde like hornes of ram :
These painted faces which they weare,
        can any tell from whence they cam ?
Don Sathan, Lord of fayned lyes
        all these new fangeles did devise."

" *Pleasant quippes for upstart newfangled gentlewomen," by Stephen Gosson*

# ROBERT DUDLEY, EARL OF LEICESTER (1588)

*Miniature by* NICHOLAS HILLIARD

*Collection of the Duke of Buccleuch and Queensberry*

" . . . and as for him t'is meete
His body's clad i' th' silkworms winding sheete."

" *The Young Gallant's Whirligig,*" *by John Taylor*

37

# HENRI III OF FRANCE (*circa* 1585)

*School of Fontainebleau*                    *Musée du Louvre*

" . . . To what good uses serve these pantofles, except it be to wear in a private house, or in a mans Chamber to keepe him warme? but to go abroad in them, as they are now used al together, is rather a let or hinderance to a man then otherwise; for shall he not be faine to knock and spurn at every stone, wall, or poste to keep them on his feet?"

" *Anatomy of Abuses,*" *by Philip Stubbes*

*Note Cordon Bleu and the cross of the Order of Saint Esprit; emblem of the Saint Esprit on left side of cloak; earring; turban; handkerchief; girdle; buttons; necklace.*

*Anonymous (c. 1585)*                    *Detail of a painting in the Musée du Louvre*

" They [women] make trunk sleeves of wyre, and whalebone bodies, backes of lathes, and stiffe bumbasted verdugals and, to the open view of all men, paint and embellish themselves with counterfeit and borrowed beauties."                    *Montaigne's Essays, tr. Florio*

" . . . And they say that the sleeves borne out with whalebones, were first invented, to avoid men's familiar touching of their armes."                    *" Itinerary " of Fynes Moryson*

*Note back view of necklace ; rebato or supportasse ; hats worn indoors.*

*From " La Première Partie du Compte de
Richard Cooke," 1584*

Coryat, having visited France, tells us about the royal
bodyguards : " [they wear] long skirted half sleeved
cotes made of white cloth, but their skirts mingled with
red and greene and the bodies of the cotes trimmed before
and behind with mayles of plaine silver, but not thick as
rich cotes of English guards."  " *Coryat's Crudities* "

*Note singers ; hatless courtiers ; Henri III wearing his
hat at table, as was the usual custom of the times ;
serving men.*

*By* MARC GHEERAERTS                    *Collection of Preston Davie, Esq., New York*
*the elder*                    *Photograph by courtesy of the Frick Art Reference Library*

" The sets of my old ruffe looked like so many organ
pipes."                    *Randolph, " Hey for Honesty "*

*Note fan ; wired veil.*

## MARY QUEEN OF SCOTS (1578)

*By* P. OUDRY

" . . . on hir head shee had a dressing of lawne edged with bone lace, and a pomander chayne and an agnus dei about hir necke, a crucifix in hir hande, a payre of beades att hir girdle, with a silver cross att the end of them.  A vale of lawne fastned to hir caule bowed out with wyer, and edged round about with boane lace . . ."   In a letter to the Right Honourable Sir William Cecil.

*" Letters of Mary Queen of Scots," by Agnes Strickland*

By FEDERIGO ZUCCARO                    *Courtesy of the Gallery of Fine Arts, Yale University*

" . . . she had on a necklace of exceeding fine jewels ; her hands were small, her fingers long, and her stature neither tall nor low ; her air was stately, her manner of speaking mild and obliging."

*Hentzner's Travels, " Progresses of Queen Elizabeth," by John Nichols*

*Note billament ; head attire ; fan.*

43

*Miniature by* ISAAC OLIVER                    *Windsor Castle*

*Reproduced by the gracious permission of His Majesty the King*

" They have also boothose which are to be wondered at ;  for they be of the fynest cloth that may be got, . . . yet this is bad inough to were next their gresie boots.  And would to God this weare all :  but (oh phy for shame !) they must be wrought all over, from the gartering place upward, with nedle worke, clogged with silk of all colours, with birds, foules, beasts and antiques purtrayed all over in comlie sorte . . ."

" *Anatomy of Abuses," by Philip Stubbes*

*Note long locks ;  very long rapier ;  gloves.*

44

*Miniature by* NICHOLAS HILLIARD          *Victoria and Albert Museum*

"... You would thinke him nothing but a swarme of Butterflies, if you saw him a far off."

"*Pierce Penilesse, his Supplication to the divell,*" *by Thomas Nashe*

*Note "peascod bellied" doublet.*

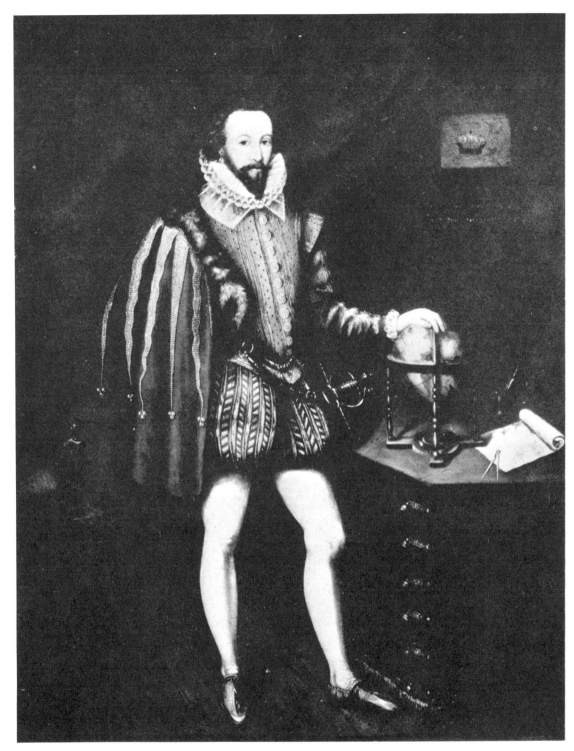

*Anonymous*     *Collection of Preston Davie, Esq., New York.   Photograph by courtesy of the Frick Art Reference Library*

" Nay, he doth wear an emblem 'bout his neck ;
For under that fair ruff so sprucely set,
Appears a fall, a falling-band forsooth . . . "
" *The Scourge of Villainy.   Satyre III,*"  *by John Marston*

" Some lustie courtiers also and gentlemen of courage doo weare
either rings of gold, stoncs, or pcarlc in their earcs . . . "
" *The Chronicles of England, Scotlande and Irelande,*" *by Raphael Holinshed*

*Note paned trunk hose ;  pinked doublet ;  razed shoes.*

" . . . 1581 . . . hir Majestie . . . entred the ship which Captaine Drake had so hapily guided round about the world—and there she did make Captaine Drake Knight . . .

" . . . In the yeere one thousand five hundred eightie and eight, he was Vice-Admiral of the whole Navie by Commission against the invincible Armado." " *The Chronicles of England, by John Stow*

ÆTATIS SVÆ LVIII
A⁰ DÑI 1591

*Anonymous*         *By permission of the Plymouth City Museum and Art Gallery Committee*

" Tobacco, was first brought, and made knowne in England by Sir John Hawkins, about the yeere one thousand five hundred sixty five, but not used by englishmen in many yeers after, though at this day commonly used by most men, and many women . . ."     *Howes' edition of Stow's " Annales of England "*

By ALONZO SANCHEZ-COELLO              *Collection of Alex. Shaw, Esq., Buenos Aires*

" The women there use great ruffes . . . then least they should fall down, they are smeared and starched in the devils liquore, I mean Starch ; after that dryed with great diligence, streaked, patted, and rubbed very nicely, and so applyed to their goodly necks, and withall, underpropped with supportasses the statelie arches of pride . . ."

*" Anatomy of Abuses," by Philip Stubbes*

*Note ruff of bone lace ; rebato or supportasse, supporting the ruff ; bolstered hair.*

49

*By* FELIPE DE LIAÑO                              *Prado, Madrid*

" . . . it is nothing but a token of fair pride to wear such vardingals . . ." "*Remains and Sermons*," *by Hugh Latimer*

*Note the earliest type or "Spanish" farthingale, funnel shape ; decorative use of points and aglets.*

*Anonymous*                                                    *Uffizi Gallery, Florence*

" Then, on toppes of these stately turrets (I meane their goodly heads wherin is more vanitie than true Philosophie now and then) stand their other capitall ornaments . . . according to the variable fantasies of their serpentine minds."

*" Anatomy of Abuses," by Philip Stubbes*

*Note bow-knot earrings.*

*From an engraving by* JOHANNES TH. DE BRY

"Although the noble women of Venice always appear so richly dressed with ornaments of gold and jewels . . . yet is this elegance surpassed in the toilette of a noble fiancée. She is dressed in cloth of gold and has upon her head a diadem of pearls and precious stones, wearing her long hair hanging loose behind over the shoulders, interwoven with threads of gold. . . "

*Franco, " Habiti delle donne Venetiane "*

*Note gentlemen of rank in their gowns and tippets and little fleece caps.*
*(See Moryson's account on page 17.)*

*Woodcut by Christopher Chrieger from " Degli Abiti Antichi e Moderni,"*
*1590, by Cesare Vecellio.*

" In Venice they construct on the roofs of their houses square erections of wood in the form of uncovered terraces, called ' belvederes,' on which all the women, or at least most of them, try assiduously to render their hair blond. By means of diverse sorts of waters or compositions made expressly, capable of enduring everything to obtain this result, they resign themselves to this occupation in the heat of the sun. They are seated and wash their hair with a little sponge attached to the end of a rod. These women wear a ' schiavonetto,' a garment of silk or light cloth and upon their heads, to protect themselves from the sun, they wear a fine hat of straw, which they call ' solana.' They hold their mirror in their hand." *" Degli Abiti Antichi e Moderni," by Cesare Vecellio.*

*Note chopines : the dressing-gown was at this period called in England " night-gown."*

53

## GEORG FRIEDRICH VON BRANDENBURG AND HIS WIFE SOPHIA

*Cistercian Abbey, Heilsbronn*

" Thy bodies bolstered out, With bumbast . . ."

" *Fables of Jeronimo,*" *by George Gascoigne.*

*By* FRANS POURBUS *the younger*                    *Collection of Mrs. Leveson-Gower, New York*

" O mercy, God ! what masquing stuff is here ?
What's this ?  a sleeve ?  'tis like a demi-cannon :
What !  up and down, carv'd like an apple-tart ?
Here's snip and nip and cut and slish and slash,
Like to a censer in a barber's shop.
Why, what, i' devils name, tailor, call'st thou this ? "

*Shakespeare, " The Taming of the Shrew," IV. iii.* 87.

*By* PAUL VAN SOMER                                          *Private collection*

"When the Queen goes abroad in public the Lord
Chamberlain walks first, being followed by all the nobility
who are in Court, and the Knights of the Order that are
present walk after, near the Queen's person, such as the
Earl of Essex, the Admiral and others."

*De Maisse* " *Journal*," 1597.

*Attributed to* LUCAS DE HEERE    *Metropolitan Museum of Art, New York*

" She wore innumerable jewels on her person, not only on her head, but also within her collar, about her arms and on her hands, with a very great quantity of pearls, round her neck and on her bracelets. She had two bands, one on each arm, which were worth a great price." *De Maisse* " *Journal*," 1597.

*Note semi-circular farthingale.*

57

*Anonymous*                    *Collection of the Duke of Devonshire, Hardwick Hall (Hanfstængl photo.)*

" High above all a cloth of State was spred,
   And a rich throne, as bright as sunny day,
   On whiche sate most brave embellished
   With royall robes and gorgeous array,
   A mayden queene, that shone as Titans ray,
   In glistring gold, and peerelesse pretious stones
   Yet her bright blazing beautie did assay
   To dim the brightnesse of her glorious throne,
   As envying her selfe, that too exceeding shone."

   " *The Faerie Queene,*" *by Edmund Spenser.*

*By* MARC GHEERAERTS *the younger*                    *Knole Collection*

" I have seen them swallow gravell, ashes, coales, dust, tallow, candles, and for the nonce, labour and toyle themselves to spoil their stomache, only to get a pale-bleake colour.  To become slender in wast, and to have a straight spagnolized body, what pinching, what girding, what cingling will they not indure ;  yea sometimes with yron-plates, with whale-bones and other such trash . . ."                    *Montaigne's Essays, tr. Florio.*

" . . . And they use a strange badge of pride, to weare little looking glasses at their girdles."                    " *Itinerary* " *of Fynes Moryson.*

*Note fan ; mirror ; head attire.*

59

*By* MARC GHEERAERTS *the elder*               *Collection of Lord de L'Isle and Dudley, Penshurst*

" With ruffs and cuffs and farthingales and things."

*Shakespeare,*" *The Taming of the Shrew,*" *IV. iii.* 56.

*Note young children in aprons.*

*By* MARC GHEERAERTS *the elder*

*Collection of Col. Wingfield-Digby, Sherborne Castle, Dorset*
*Photograph by courtesy of The Witt Library, London*

" This day se'night her Majestie was at Blackfriars to grace the marriage of Lord Harbert and his wife.   The bride met the Queen at the waterside, where my Lord Cobham had provided a lectica made like a litter, whereon she was carried to my Lady Russell's by six knights."　　　　　*R. Whyte to Sir R. Sidney, June 23rd, 1600.*

Bearing sword before the Queen, Lord Cobham ; foreground, the father of the groom ; last litter-bearer, Lord Herbert, the bridegroom ; behind him, Anne Russell, the bride.

*Note the knights in their chains, and their garter on the left leg ; the Queen and the bride with throat bare, while the married ladies wear closed ruffs.*

*Anonymous engraving of the early seventeenth century*

" A Buske, a Maske, a Fanne, a monstrous Ruffe,
" A boulster for their Buttockes and such stuffe."

" *Satyres,*" *by Samuel Rowlands,* 1600.

*Painting on wood by an unknown artist*                                        *Collection of the late C. B. King, Esq., London*

" Theyr breasts they embuske up on hie and theyr round
Roseate buds immodestly lay foorth, and shew at their handes
there is fruit to be hoped . . ."

" *Christ's Teares over Jerusalem,*" *by Thomas Nashe.*

*From " Habiti delle donne Venetiane,"* 1610, *by* GIACOMO FRANCO

[Speaking of a Venetian courtesan] " In her cheeks thou shalt see the Lilly and the Rose strive for supremacy, in that curious manner besides her low frilled peakes standing up like prety pyrimids, that they give thee the true cose amoris." " Many of them which have an elegant naturel beauty, doe varnish their faces (the observation whereof made me not a little pitty their vanities) with these kinde of sordid trumperies." *" Coryat's Crudities."*

" Their dublettes are noe lesse monstrous than the reste ; For now the fashion is to have them hang downe in the middest of their theighes or at least to their privie members, being so hardequilted and stuffed, bombasted and sewed, as they can verie hardly eyther stoupe downe or decline them selves to the grounde, soe styffe and sturdy they stand about them." " *Anatomy of Abuses,"* by *Philip Stubbes.*

" . . . . wide saucy sleeves that would be in every dish before their master."
*" The Truth of our Times,"* by *Henry Peacham.*

64

*Engraving by* JAN WIERIX

" Then followeth the trimming and tricking of their heds in laying out their heir to the shewe, which of force must be curled, frisled and crisped, laid out (a World to see) on wreathes and borders from one ear to an other, and least it should fall down, it is underpropped with forks, wyers and I can not tel what, rather like grime sterne monsters, then chaste christian matrones.  Then on the edges of their bolstred heir . . . there is layd great wreathes of gold and silver, curiouslie wrought and cunninglie applied to the temples of their heads.  And for fear of lacking any thing to set foorth their pride withal, at their heyre, thus wreathed and crested, are hanged bugles (I dare not say bables) ouches, rings, gold, silver, glasses, and such other childishe gewgawes and foolish trinckets besides, which, for they are innumerable, and I, unskillfull in wemens termes, I can not easily recount.  But God give them grace to give over these vanities, and studie to adorn their heads with the incorruptible ornaments of virtue and true Godlynesse." " *Anatomy of Abuses," by Philip Stubbes.*

*Note bobbin or bone lace with purle edge ;  billament ;  carcanet ;  buttons.*

*Engraving by* JAN WIERIX

" . . . Fardingales above the Loynes to waire,
That be she near so bombe-thin, yet she crosse like seems four squaire,"
*" Albion's England," by W. Warner, as quoted by F. W. Fairholt.*

" . . . the blocke for his heade alters faster then the Feltmaker can
fitte him, and therupon we are called in scorne *Blockheads*. And
thus we that mocke everie Nation, for keeping one fashion yet steale
patches from everie one of them, to peece out our pride, are now
laughing-stocks to them, because their cut so scurvily becomes us."
*" The Seven Deadly Sinnes of London," by Thomas Dekker.*

*Note breeches open at the knee ; cuirass.*

*Engraving by* R. ELSTRACKE

" . . . Five hours ago I set a dozen maids to attire a boy like a nice gentle-woman ; but there is such doing with their looking glasses, pinning, unpinning, setting, unsetting, formings and conformings, painting blew veins and cheeks ; such stirr with sticks and combs, cascanets, dressings, purls, falls, squares, busks, bodies, scarfs, necklaces, carcanets, rebatoes, borders, tires, fans, palisadoes, puffs, ruffs, cuffs, muffs, pusles, fusles, partlets, frislets, bandlets, fillets, crosslets, pendulets, amulets, annulets, bracelets, and so many lets [hindrances] that yet she is scarce dressed to the girdle ; and now there's such a calling for fardingales, kirtles, busk-points, shoe ties, etc., that seven peddlers' shops—nay all Stourbridge fair—will scarce furnish her : A ship is sooner rigged by far, than a gentlewoman made ready."    "*Lingua, or the combat of the tongue,*" *by Thomas Tomkis.*

*Note kirtle ; shoe roses ; lesser Geórge on ribbon ; rope of beads worn baldrick-wise.*

*Engraving, probably by* R. ELSTRACKE

"They strangle and cloke more velvet in a deep-gathered hose, than would serve to line through my lord What-call-ye-him's coach." "*The Blacke Booke,*" *by Thomas Middleton.*

". . . With two Provincial roses on my razed shoes."

*Shakespeare, "Hamlet," III, ii, 294.*

*Note coronet.*

*Engraving by* SIMON VAN DE PASS *from John Smith's " General Historie of Virginia "*

" . . . Pocahontas . . . by the diligent care of Master John Rolfe her husband and his friends, was taught to speake such English as might well bee understood, well instructed in Christianitie, and was become very formall and civill after our English manner."

" *General Historie of Virginia,*" *by Captain John Smith,* 1624.

Anonymous

Metropolitan Museum of Art, New York

" Surely the Italians in generall respect convenience more then ornament of their apparrell."

" *Itinerary* " *of Fynes Moryson*

*Note flowers over the ear.*

*By* MARC GHEERAERTS *the younger*                    *Courtesy of M. Knoedler & Co.*

" . . . to feede the fantasticall pride of our youth, in new Stuffes . . ."

" *Itinerary* " *of Fynes Moryson.*

By MARC GHEERAERTS *the younger*      *By the courtesy of The Witt Library*

" . . . why is all this rigging and fine tackle, mistress . . ."

" *The Devil is an Ass,*" by Ben Jonson.

*Note. The fanciful attire and the wearing of flowers*
*would indicate festivities in connection with a marriage*
*celebration.*

*By* DANIEL MYTENS *the elder*

" . . . 'fore hell, my heart was at my mouth,
'Till I had view'd his shoes well : for those roses
were big enough to hide a cloven foot."

" *The Devil is an Ass*," by Ben Jonson.

*Note hat ; garters ; heels.*

PORTRAIT OF A GENTLEMAN (EARLY XVIIth CENTURY)

*Miniature by* NICHOLAS HILLIARD          *Collection of the Duke of Portland*

" Playing with some string of your band which is a most quaint
kind of melancholy besides."

*" Cynthia's Revels," by Ben Jonson,* 1601.

*Note cord bracelet with ring attached ; pickadil collar support.*

*By* MARC GHEERAERTS
*the younger*

*Victoria and Albert Museum. Photograph*
*by courtesy of H. Clifford Smith, Esq.*

" And herby it appeareth that no people in the World are so curiouse
in new fangles as they of England be."

*Anatomy of Abuses," by Philip Stubbes.*

*Note " bobbin " or " bone " lace.*

*By* PAUL VAN SOMER          *National Portrait Gallery*

Knights of the Garter

" The habit of these Knights is an undergarment or gowne of crimson velvet of some called a kirtle, over which he weareth a mantle of purple velvet lined with white sarsnet, on the left shoulder thereof is embroidered in a garter an Eschuchion of S. George, and over his right shoulder hangeth his hood of crimson velvet lined with white, the cordons of the mantle are purple silk and gold. Above all which, about his necke he weareth the collar of the order, being of pure gold, made of garters and knots, and enamiled with roses white and red, weying 30 ounces of Troy weight, with the image of S. George, richly garnished with precious stones, pendant thereat. About his left legge he weareth buckled a garter enriched with gold, pearle and stones, whereupon these French words are embrodered, *Hony soit qui mally pense.* Which may be thus Englished, shame be to him that evill thinketh."

*" Honor Military and Civill," by W. Segar.*

*Note cork-soled shoes ; cap ; white staff.*

*Miniature by* ISAAC OLIVER          *Victoria and Albert Museum*

" Then have they nether-stocks to these gay hosen, not of cloth . . . for that is thought to base . . . and so curiouslye knit with open seam down the leg, with quirks and clocks about the ancles, and sometime (haply) interlaced with gold or silver threds, as is wunderful to behold."

" *Anatomy of Abuses,*" *by Philip Stubbes*

By FRANS POURBUS *the younger*                    *Prado, Madrid*

"Lawn as white as driven snow;
Cyprus black as e'er was crow."

*Shakespeare, " A Winter's Tale," IV. iii.* 220.

*Note rare example of closed ruff not covering the throat.*

*By* FRANS POURBUS *the younger*    *Prado, Madrid*

" They shew the swellings of their mind, in the swellings
and plumping out of theyr apparrayle."

" *Christ's Teares over Jerusalem," by Thomas Nashe*

*Note ruff* " *à la confusion* " *; pinked and slashed or razed fabric.*

Selections from "The Procession at the Obsequies of Sir Philip Sidney," drawn by his servant, Thomas Lant, and engraved by Th. Dirk de Bry, 1587. (*From the series of three hundred and forty-four engraved figures in the possession of the Folger Shakespeare Library, Washington, D.C.*)

*Engraving by* CRISPIN VAN DE PASS *the younger from Antoine de Pluvinel's* "*Instruction du Roy*"

The King (Louis XIII) : "How should one on horseback be attired?"
Pluvinel (riding master) : "It is not my desire, Sir, to refrain anyone
from attiring himself otherwise than according
to his fancy, knowing that all men of good
judgement will seek that which is proper, and in
so doing, will find their comfort."

"*L'Instruction du Roy en l'exercise de monter à cheval,*" *by Antoine de Pluvinel.*

*Note, that as costume now develops toward a new era, the doublet becomes somewhat concave breasted, and the hair is worn longer.*

*Anonymous*          *Collection of the Duke of Richmond and Gordon, Goodwood.*   *Photograph by courtesy of The Witt Library*

Lord Treasurer
Justice                    Justice
Surveyor                    Attorney
Queen's Serjeant                              Counsel, pleading
Receiver General                    Auditor
Usher                    Messenger, wearing
royal arms

Outside the bar are two Serjeants in white
coifs, the one at the left having been recently
appointed as may be seen by his parti-
coloured gown.

*Anonymous*　　　　　　　　　　　　　　　　　　　　　　　*National Portrait Gallery*

" Judges in term are to sit at Westminster in the Courts in their
Black or Violet Gowns whether they will ; and a Hood of the
same colour . . . and their mantles above all ; the end of the Hood
hanging over behind ; wearing their Velvet Caps, and Coyfes of
Lawn and cornered caps . . . then Judges begin to wear their Robes
faced with white fur of Minever " [according to season].

" *Origines Juridiciales,*" *by W. Dugdale,* 1671.

*Anonymous*　　　　　　　　　　　　　　　　　　　　*Uffizi Gallery, Florence*

" . . . long mantles, made after fashion of those which are worne the day of S. Michael, of black velvet embrodered all about with gold and silver, and embroderie made of flowers de Liesse, and knots of gold, betweene the sundry cyphers of silver, and flambes of gold seamed . . . Upon the said mantles they openly weare the great collar of the order . . ."

*" Honor Military and Civill," by W. Segar.*

*(For a full account of this ceremonial attire and that of other important orders of the period, see the above work)*

*Note, above the collar of St. Esprit the King is wearing the collar of St. Michael.*

*Madonna and Child appearing to St. John, by* GIAMBATTISTA MORONI. *Trento*

The Pope is wearing his tiara, the Cardinal his scarlet hat,
and the two bishops their mitres.

*Note monials ; crosier ; pontificals.*

85

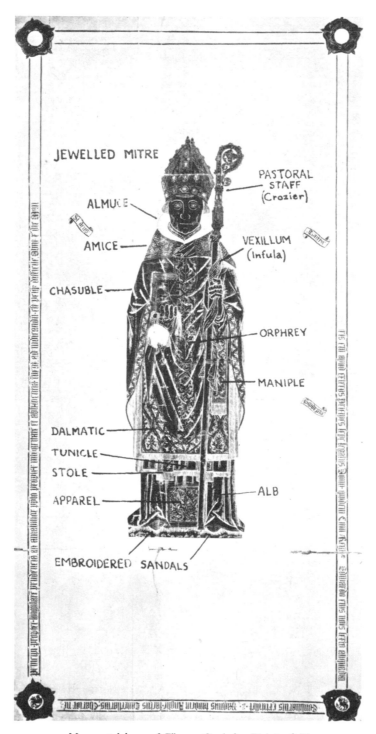

JEWELLED MITRE

PASTORAL STAFF (Crozier)

ALMUCE

AMICE

VEXILLUM (Infula)

CHASUBLE

ORPHREY

MANIPLE

DALMATIC

TUNICLE

STOLE

APPAREL

ALB

EMBROIDERED SANDALS

*Monumental brass of Thomas Goodryke, Bishop of Ely*

Mitre is jewelled, the infulæ not visible

Amice is apparelled, as is the skirt of the alb

Chasuble (plain) with ornamented border and an embroidered pillar orphrey

Dalmatic (figured) fringed at bottom and sides

Tunicle, fringed, is of plain material

Stole is between dalmatic and tunicle

Maniple is embroidered the whole length

Pastoral staff

Vexillum (infula) is the scarf attached to the staff

Sandals embroidered

Almuce appears to be worn under the Mass vestments, part of it showing round neck above amice.

*See H. J. Clayton, " Ornaments of the Ministers."*

*Detail from the Burial of the Conde Orgaz, by* EL GRECO        *Toledo*

" Set down, set down your honourable load,
If honour may be shrouded in a hearse."

*Shakespeare, " Richard III," I. ii.* 1.

*Note orphreys on cope and dalmatic.*

## CARDINAL DON FERNANDO (*circa* 1596)

*By* EL GRECO                    *Metropolitan Museum of Art, New York*

" In all places of the world there be not so many that walk in the streets converse and eate in spectacles. As in this town you cannot meete tenne but you shall find one of them with a paire of glass eyes." "*Notes from Spain,*" *by Sir Richard Wynne in Nichols' "Progresses of King James I.*"

*Note mozetta ; biretta ; pontificals.*

*By* FEDERIGO ZUCCARO          *Courtesy of the Frick Art Reference Library*

Parliamentary Robes. "The mantle of the baron had two bars of miniver with borders of gold lace, and the viscount had two and one half bars. The mantle of the baron and the viscount opened on the right side with the distinguishing bars of fur on the right shoulder only. The mantle of all others opened in front and had capes of fur covering both shoulders."

*Augustin Vincent, MSS.* 151, *in the College of Arms,* 1622 *(Planché)*

*Note gloves.*

*By* ROWLAND LOCKEY                                        *Collection of the Earl of Verulam. Gorhambury*

"Bishops never appearing publickly but in their rochets, nor officiating otherwise than in copes at the holy altar."

"*History of the Reformation of the Church of England,*" *by Peter Heylyn,* 1560.

*By* HANS EWARTH                    *Collection of the Earl of Radnor, Longford Castle*

" And is not a buff jerkin a most sweet robe of durance ? "

*Shakespeare,* " 1*st Henry IV,*" *I. ii.* 48.

*Note, the jerkin here illustrated may be of a leather more pliable than* " *buff.*"    *Comb morion ;*
*powder flask or primer (* " *touch-box* ").

*Tapestry designed by* FRANÇOIS QUESNEL          *Uffizi Gallery, Florence*

Roger de Hoveden describes the tournament as a " military exercise carried out not in the spirit of hostility but solely for practice and the display of prowess."

" *Glossarium,*" *of Charles du Fresne du Gange.*

The tapestry depicts not the tournament (in which the contestants are mounted and tilt across a solid barrier), but here the play is at " barriers," in which they tilt afoot across an open barrier.

*Note the Swiss Guards in the background. For Coryat's amusing observations upon the Swiss Guards at the French court, see page 15. See also page 11 for a description of " Sir Philip Sidney and the Tournament."*

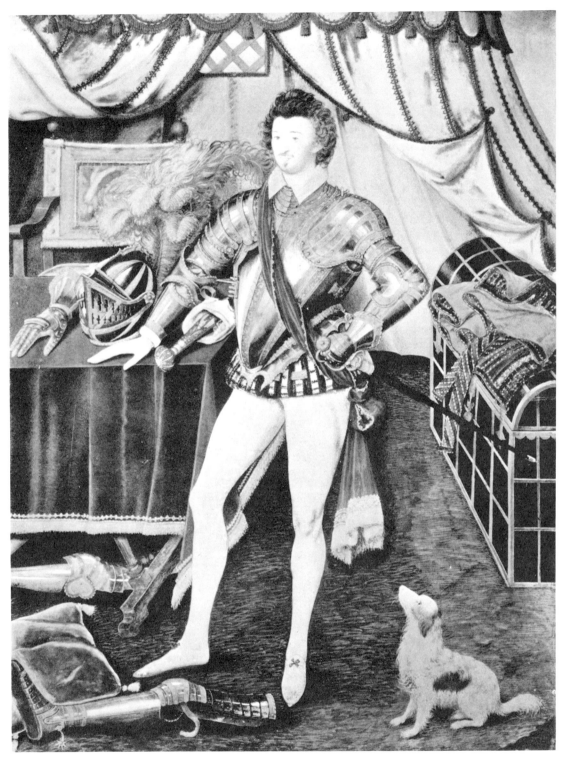

*Miniature by* ISAAC OLIVER                    *Cleveland Museum of Art, Cleveland, Ohio*

" I had great preparation of armour, as well of proofe, as of light
corsletts, yet not a man would use them, but esteemed a pott of
wine a better defence than an armour of proofe . . ."
" *Voiage into the South Sea,*" *by Sir Richard Hawkins.*

*Note "peascod bellied" breast plate.*

# ARMOUR OF GEORGE CLIFFORD (Made *circa* 1591)

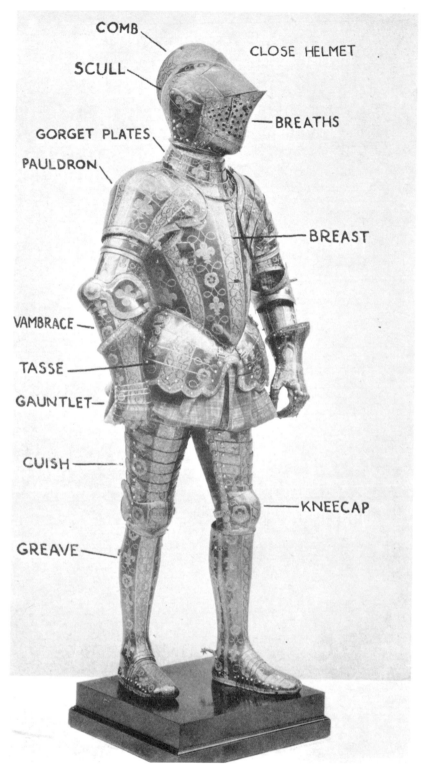

*Metropolitan Museum of Art, New York*

" Like a rich armour worn in heat of day,
    That scalds with safety."

*Shakespeare, " 2nd Henry IV," IV. v. 29.*

# GEORGE CLIFFORD, 3rd EARL OF CUMBERLAND (*circa* 1590)

*Miniature by* NICHOLAS HILLIARD    *Collection of the Duke of Buccleuch and Queensberry*

" . . . This noble gentleman (George Clifford) by her majesties expresse commandement is yerely (without respect unto his age) personally present at these military exercises, there to see, survey, and as one most carefull and skilfull to direct them."     " *Honor Military and Civill," by William Segar.*

George Clifford distinguished himself among the commanders of the fleet opposed to the Spanish Armada in 1588. Elizabeth bestowed her glove upon him, and he wore it ever after in front of his hat at public ceremonies.

Indi cuiuſdam Gnomologia inſignis de Chri-    XXI.
ſtianorum auaritia.

P ANCHIACO *Regulus amicitia cum* Valboa *contracta, illi grandem au-*
*ri vim elaborati in vaſa & monilia, dat. Uerum conſpicatus Hiſpanos,*
*dum aurum hoc penditur, inter ſe rixari, & eductis gladijs ſeſe mutuo fe-*
*rire velle, aurum cum trutina euertit, illorum auaritiam acerbe carpens.*
*Atq, ſi tanta auri cupiditate arderent, regiones demonſtraturum in qui-*
*bus abundantiſſime id inuenirent.* Valboam *deinde per difficilia itinera ad ſumma mon-*
*tium iuga deducit è quibus mare Auſtrale ipſi demonſtrat. Reuerſus Pan-*
*chiacum baptiſandum curat & Carolum*
*nuncupat.*

F  2          *Valboa*

*Engraving by* DIRK DE BRY *for "* Collectiones Peregrinationum in Indiam Orientalem et Occidentalem*,"* 1594

A late sixteenth-century conception of early sixteenth-century
history.   The costumes are of the Elizabethan period.

*Tapestry*                                                      *Spanish State Property*

" . . . the sleightest armour secureth the parts of a mans body, which it covereth from pike, sword and all hand weapons, it likewise giveth boldnesse and courage ; a man armed giveth a greater and waightier blow than a man unarmed, he standeth faster, and with great difficultie is to be overthrown."

" *Voiage into the South Sea,*" *by Sir Richard Hawkins.*

*Note Spanish morion (cabasset) ; various types of breeches.*

*Engraving from* J. DE GHEYN's " *Maniement d'Armes,*" 1608

"... I think them to be verie maniable weapons, for such soldiers as are well practiced, and do know how to use them ..." " *Certain Discourses,*" *by Sir John Smythe.*

*Engraving from* J. DE GHEYN's " *Maniement d'Armes,*" 1608

" The armes of a Musquetier offensive are a Musquet . . .
Bandoleer with 12 charges at the least, primer, bullet bag and
pruning yron, with a Rest of a length proportionable to his
stature, and a sword.   As for the defensive armes, he hath
none, although in some parts I have seene them weare a Head
peace."  "*Militarie Instructions for the Learned,*" *by Thomas Kellie.*

*Engraving from* J. DE GHEYN's " *Maniement d'Armes,*" 1608

" Armes which our Pike-men are accostomed to carrie are : a
Head-peace, or Morion, a Gorget or craige-peace, a Corslet, or
cuirace with Taces ; I have seene some weare Puldrons or arme
Pyces, and those are defensive : his offensive armes are a Sword,
and Picke of 15 foote long . . ."

" *Militarie Instructions for the Learned,*" *by Thomas Kellie.*

# GLOSSARY

*Wherein is set forth the meaning of words concerning costume of the following orders :* CIVIL, PROFESSIONAL, CEREMONIAL, ECCLESIASTICAL *and* MILITARY

The Glossary has been compiled from a great many sources of which the following have been an indispensable aid :—

> Bartlett's *Concordance to Shakespeare*
> Cotgrave's *Dictionarie*.
> Druitt's *Costume on Brasses*.
> Fairholt's *Costume in England*.
> Florio's *A Worlde of Wordes*.
> *Encyclopædia Britannica*.
> Halliwell's *Dictionary*.
> *Oxford English Dictionary*.
> Onions, *A Shakespeare Glossary*.
> Planché's *Cyclopædia of Costume*.
> Minsheu's *Guide unto Tongues*.
> Pollard's *Short Title Catalogue*.

(See pages 126 and 127 for a complete list of authors and works cited, and for a list of books especially recommended for costume study.)
I have endeavoured to give specific acknowledgments throughout this work, but I wish here to express my profound gratitude to all those archæologists who, through their scholarly research, have made this compilation possible.

In quoting from contemporary texts, the spelling direct from first editions has been retained, wherever recourse to such rarities has been possible. H K. M.

AGLET—AIGLET. A metal sheath or tag attached to the end of lacings and used for fastening garments together. This method was commonly employed instead of buttons, hooks and eyes, although these were also in use.

ALB. A garment usually of white linen and with close-fitting sleeves. It was the second vestment put on by the priest when preparing for the celebration of Mass. It had a hole through which the head passed, and when girded at the waist, just cleared the ground. It was worn by bishop, priest, deacon and sub-deacon under the other vestments at Mass and at functions connected therewith. In England after the Reformation, the alb was ordered out of use with other " Mass Vestments." See APPAREL. See illus. on page 86.

ALDERMAN'S ATTIRE. " Over these coats hung great golden chains." See Von Klarwill's *Queen Elizabeth and some Foreigners.*

ALMAIN RIVET. A suit of light half armour fashioned with a splint breast and back.

> Davies, in 1619, said : ". . . light armed pikes, which onely have the fore-part of a corslet, and a head-peece, as is the almaine rivet . . ." (*England's Trainings.*)

> "Almaine or alman rivets—a certaine kinde of armour, or corslet for the body of a man, with the sleeves or braces of maile, or plates of iron, for the defense of the armes, so called because they be rivetteed or buckled after the old Alman fashion." (Minsheu, *Guide unto Tongues,* 1617.)

> "6 pair of Alman rivets complete, with splints, sallets, and all things thereunto belonging." (Will of Lord Barnes, 1532. Nicholas, *Testamenta Vestusta,* 1826.)

ALMUCE — AUMUCE — AMYS — AMESS — " GREY AMICE." A processional or choral vestment, and originally a fur or fur-lined hooded cape. It became at this period a fur shoulder cape with long ends hanging in front. The almuce was usually bordered by pendant tails of fur. It was worn under the cope or when the cope was omitted. In England it was known as the " grey amice " from the ordinary colour of the fur. According to the canons of 1571, it was decreed that ". . . nor any of yt order, by what name soever they be called shall hereafter weare the graye amice." (Cardwell, *Synodalia,* 1824.) See illus. on page 86.

AMICE. Liturgical vestment in the form of a rectangular piece of linen, 36 by 25 inches, usually ornamented on its upper border with a strip of decoration (APPAREL) forming a sort of stiff collar appearing above the chasuble or dalmatic. It was worn by bishop, deacon and priest. In reference to the Church of England and its supposed vestment reforms, De Maisse in his journal of 1597 writes " The cannons wear the amice and surplice as also the others . . . " See illus. on page 86.

ANAPES. See FUSTIAN.

ANIMA. Armour with back and breast of horizontal lames. (F. Kelly.)

ANLET—ANNULET—ANNELET. A ring, such as one of the rings of which mail armour was composed.

APPAREL. Strips or squares of embroidery, often very elaborate, placed as decoration upon the alb and on the amice. See illus. on pages 86 and 87.

APPRENTICES' ATTIRE. Regulations for the Apparel of London Apprentices, 1582.

> ". . . That from thenceforth no apprentice whatsoever should presume, 1. To wear any apparel but what he receives from his master. 2. To wear no hat within the city and liberty thereof, nor any thing instead thereof, but a woollen cap, without any silk in or about the same. 3. To wear no ruffles, cuffs, loose collar, nor other thing than a ruff at the collar, and that only of a yard and a half long. 4. To wear no doublets but what were made of canvas, fustian, sackcloth, English leather, or woollen cloth, and without being enriched with any manner of gold, silver, or silk. 5. To wear no other coloured cloth, or kersey, in hose or stockings, than white, blue, or russet. 6. To wear little breeches, of the same stuffs as the doublets, and without being stitched, laced, or bordered. 7. To wear a plain upper coat of cloth or leather, without pinking, stitching, edging, or silk about it. 8. To wear no other surtout than a cloth gown or cloak, lined or faced with cloth, cotton, or bays, with a fixed round collar, without stitching, guarding, lace, or silk. 9. To wear no pumps, slippers, nor shoes, but of English leather, without being pinked, edged, or stitched ; nor girdles, nor garters, other than of crewel, woollen thread, or leather, without being garnished. 10. To wear no sword, dagger, or other weapon, but a knife ; nor a ring, jewel of gold, nor silver, nor silk in any part of his apparel." (Nichols, *Progresses of Queen Elizabeth.*)

APRON—APORNE—NAPRON. An apron often of leather was worn by workmen. Women also wore aprons, but not only for utilitarian purposes. The idle gentlewoman wore, as costume accessory, an apron, often extremely fine and rich in decoration, and usually long and narrow in form. See illustrations on pages 22 and 60.

ARCHBISHOP'S VESTMENTS. An illustration of an archbishop of the Catholic Church may be seen on page 87, and of the Reformed Church on page 90. See also BISHOP, CROSIER, PALL.

ARCHER. " Necessarie it is that everie man have a good and meete Bowe according to his draught and strength light and easie, a jacke with a skull, sword and dagger, nothing upon his arms, whereby in time of service he maie easilie draw the arrow to the head, that they maie deliver the same with strength and arte as Englishmen are accustomed. They must have also a braser and shooting gloves, their stringes whipped and waxed over with glew, their feathers drie, so be they serviceable in anie weather and serve against the enemie." (Thomas Styward, *The Pathwaie to Martiall Discipline,* 1581.)

> Sir John Smythe in 1590 says, in defence of the bow, the use of which was fast giving way to fire arms, " Archers are able to discharge foure or five arrowes apeece, before the Harquebusiers shall bee readie to discharge one bullet." (*Certain Discourses.*) See BOW, CROSS-BOW.

ARCUBUS. See HARQUEBUS.

ARMAZINE. A kind of taffeta.

ARMET. Horseman's headpiece consisting of a round topped helmet with a one-pieced face guard. It was at this period used principally in the tilt yard.

ARMING " BOLSTER." Padding at the waist under the armour.

ARMING DOUBLET. A garment worn under the armour as a padding. It was made of leather, of canvas or fustian and sometimes quilted.

ARMING POINTS. Short ends of strong twine with points like laces. They were fixed principally under the armpits and bending of the arms and knees to fasten the gussets of mail, which defended those parts of the body otherwise exposed. (Meyrick.) They were later affixed to the shoulders of the buff coat for the attachment of the vambraces.

ARMOUR. " Our armour differeth not from that of other nations, and therefore consisteth of corslets, almaine rivets, shirts of maile, jackes . . . of which there is no towne or village that hath not hir convenient furniture. The said armour and munition likewise is kept in one severall place (of everie towne) appointed by the consent of the whole parish, where it is alwaies readie to be had and worne within an houres warning." (Harrison's *Description of England in Shakspere's Youth* ; 1577-1587.)

> Owing to improvements in fire arms, armour, to be bullet proof, was obliged to be so heavily constructed as

to render it almost unbearable. See PROOF ARMOUR.
" Like a rich armour worn in heat of day,
   That scalds with safety."
(Shakespeare, 2nd *Henry IV*—IV. V. 29-30.)

Armour began at this time to fall gradually into
disuse. By the process of elimination of one part after
another, armour became, after the first quarter of the
seventeenth century, practically extinct, except for the
wearing of a headpiece and gorget or cuirass. (Markham
in his *Soldier's Accidence*, 1625, favours the retention of
more full equipment.)

For TOURNAMENT ARMOUR, see illus. on pages 92,
94 and 95.

For the many parts of armour, see under their various
headings.

**BAIZE.** See BAYS.

**BALDRICK—BAUDRICKE.** A belt, girdle, or scarf
worn from one shoulder across breast and back and
under the opposite arm. It occasionally served an
ornamental purpose, but was primarily for military use
as a mark of differentiation : " Such surgeons must
wear their baldricke, whereby they may be known in
the time of slaughter." (Ralph Smith's MSS, temps.
Elizabeth, as quoted by Planché.) See illus. on pages
91 and 93. See SCARF.

**BAND.** A general term for collar, but principally the
plain turn-over collar. The band might also apply to
the shirt or doublet collar.
See FALL RUFF, SUPPORTASSE.

**BAND STRINGS.** Laces or strings attached at the
opening of band or ruff, which tie together, thus securing
the band about the neck. See illus. on page 74.

**BANDILEER—BANDOLIER.** Leather baldricks worn
by musketeers over the left shoulder. " Soldiers . . .
hang upon their neckes upon a baudricke . . . certain
pipes, which they call charges, of copper and tin, made
with covers, which they think in skirmish to bee the
more readie way." (Edw. Davies, *England's Trainings*,
1619.) See illus. on page 99.

**BARBE.** A barbe was worn primarily by widows and by
vowesses, and consisted of a white linen bib-like covering
for the throat usually pleated. It was worn tied above
or under the chin. In the famous Clouet portrait of
Mary Stuart, she is seen wearing a barbe and white
mourning for her first husband, François II. According
to contemporary account, barbes were worn by the
ladies at Mary's funeral. (See Nichols, *Progresses of Queen
Elizabeth*.) There is no evidence of their having been
worn at the funeral of Queen Elizabeth, 16 years later.
(See H. Nicholas, *Testamenta Vestusta*, 1826). See
NUNS.

**BASES.** Skirts, often pleated, and made of rich material.
They extended from waist to knee and were worn over
armour. Bases, though much worn in earlier periods,
are rarely seen at this time, excepting possibly as a part
of tournament attire.
" By your furtherance I am cloth'd in steel . .
   Only, my friend, I yet am unprovided
   Of a pair of bases."
(Shakespeare, *Pericles*—II. I. 166.)

**BASQUINE—VASQUINE.** Spanish word for petticoat.
See FARTHINGALE.

**BATTLE-AXE.** " Short weapons being Bils, which I call
Battle-axes." (Sir John Smythe, *Certain Discourses*,
1590.)

**BATON—BASTON.** See STAFF OF OFFICE.

**BAUDEKIN.** " Bawdkin or tynsell." (Baret, *Dictionarie*,
1580.)
A rich fabric probably a sort of brocade woven of
silk and gold thread. " Arraied in cloth of gold of the
most pretious and costly Bawdkin." (Holland's tr. of
Camden's *Britannia*, 1610.)

**BAVERETTE.** " A bib, mocket or mocketer to put
before the bosome of a slavering child." (Cotgrave,
1611.)

**BAYONNETTE.** " A kind of small flat pocket-dagger
furnished with knives ; or a great knife to hang at the
girdle like a dagger." (Cotgrave, 1611.)

**BAYS—BAIZE.** " A coarse woollen manufacture ; fab-
ricated in England at Colchester during the reign of
Elizabeth, and occasionally used for the garments of
country people." (Fairholt.)

**BEADLE.** " . . . The three Esquire Beadles did give
their attendance upon hir Majestie's person as oft as she
went abroad in state, and had place next before the
serjeants at arms beinge in chaines of gold, and in fayre
gownes . . . "
The Queen at Oxford, 1592. (Nichols' *Progresses of
Queen Elizabeth*.)

**BEADS.** Used for ornamentation and as a rosary for
prayer. They were made of glass, amber, metal and
wood and compositions of various kinds.
" With amber bracelets, beads and all this knavery."
(Shakespeare, *Taming of the Shrew*—IV. III. 58.)

**BEARD.** Unless a man were very young, he would in all
probability have worn a beard of almost any conceiv-
able cut.
" Some seeme as they were starched stiffe and fine,
Like to the bristles of some angry swine ;
And some (to set their Love's desire on edge)
Are cut and prun'd like to a quickset hedge.
Some like a spade, some like a forke, some square,
Some round, some mow'd like stubble, some starke
             bare,
Some sharpe, Stiletto fashion, dagger like,
That may with whispering a man's eyes outpike :
Some with the hammer cut, or Romane T,
Their beards extravagant reform'd must be,
Some with the quadrate, some triangle fashion,
Some circular, some ovall in translation,
Some perpendicular in longitude,
Some like a thicket for their crassitude,
That heights, depths, bredths, triforme, square,
             ovall, round,
And rules Geometricall in beards are found."
(John Taylor in his *Superbiæ Flagellum*, 1621.)
See page 26.

**BEARING CLOTH.** A robe or cloth used for covering
a child when carried to baptism.
" A bearing cloth for a squire's child."
(Shakespeare, *Winter's Tale*—III. III. 18.)

**BEAVER.** (*a*) At this period the beaver was the movable
face guard of a close helmet. It was composed of two
sections : the buffe or nether beaver, covering the chin,
and the ventaille or upper beaver with breathing holes.
(F. M. Kelly.) The latter section could move up or down,
thus exposing the face. The beaver could also include
the visor, or uppermost section of the faceguard.
" I'll hide my silver beard in a gold beaver."
(Shakespeare, *Troilus*—I. III. 296.)
See illus. on page 94. See BUFFE.
(*b*) A hat made of beaver fur or some imitation thereof.

**BELT.** See GIRDLE.

**BIB.** See BAVARETTE, MOCKETER.

**BIGGON—BIGGIN.** A child's cap. A hood. Also
the coif of a serjeant-at-law.
" As he whose brow with homely biggin bound
Snores out the watch of night."
(Shakespeare, 2nd *Henry IV*—IV. V. 26.)

**BILBO.** A sword of Bilbao at which Spanish town fine
steel blades were manufactured.

**BILL.** Military pole arm consisting of a staff not more
than six feet in length topped by a sort of spiked axe
blade. A " brown bill " is one that is either rusty or
painted brown to avoid the necessity of polishing. They
were at times painted black.
" . . . the Bills must bee of good stuffe, not like our
common browne Bills, which are lightlie for the most
part all yron, with a little steele or none at all ; but they
ought to bee made of good yron and steele, with long

strong pikes at the least of 12 inches long, armed with yron at the midds of the staffe, like the Holberts, for example, like unto those which the Earle of Leicester, and Sir William Pelham had in the Low Countries for their guards, being made thus, no doubt, but it is a necessarie weapon to guard Ensignes in the field, Trenches or Townes, and a good weapon to execute . . . "

(Sir Roger Williams, *Briefe Discourse of Warre*, 1590.)
" My brain-pan had been cleft with a brown bill."

(Shakespeare, 2nd *Henry VI*—IV. X. 13.)

A form of bill was also carried by watchmen, probably the brown bill.  See HALBARD.

BILLAMENT—BILLIMENT.  " Billementes—the attire or ornaments of a woman's head or necke ; as a bonet, a french hoode, a paste or such like." (Baret, 1580.)

BILLEMENT LACE.  See LACE.

BILLMEN, also called " bills."  " . . . These be armed with corslettes and be placed in the heart of the battaile, usuallie called the slaughter of the field . . " (T. Styward, *Pathwaie to Martiall Discipline*, 1581.)

BINDING CLOTH.  See CROSS-CLOTH.

BIRETTA.  " Barret-cap "—a non liturgical cap worn by catholic ecclesiastics, such as cardinal, bishop, prelate and priest. See illus. on page 88. See PILEUS.

BISHOP'S FUNCTIONS AND INSIGNIA.  Besides the full functions of the priesthood, bishops have the sole right (1) to confer holy orders, (2) to administer confirmation, (3) to prepare the holy oil or chrism, (4) to consecrate sacred places or utensils, (5) to give benediction to abbots and abbesses, (6) to anoint kings. (*Encyclopædia Britannica*, 14th Edit.)

Insignia for mass—cassock, amice, alb, stole, maniple, chasuble, dalmatic, tunicle, buskins, sandals, gloves, ring, mitre, pastoral staff.

Insignia for processions or choir—cassock, surplice, almuce, cope, etc.

Besides the above mass vestments, the archbishop had the cross staff and the pall.

See illus. on page 85.

The anglican bishop may be seen on page 90.

Heylyn in his *History of the Reformation*, 1661, says, " These Bishops [Parker, etc.] never appearing publickly but in their rochets, nor officiating otherwise than in copes at the holy alter." (*Hierurgia Anglicana*.) See ROBE.

BLACKING.  Shoe polish.  " . . . can make your mastership's shoes as black as ink." (Peele's *The Old Wives' Tale*, 1595.)

BODKIN.  (*a*) A dagger.
" When he himself might his quietus make
With a bare bodkin."

(Shakespeare, *Hamlet*—III. I. 76.)

(*b*) Hair ornament in the shape of a long pin with a decorative top.  Among the New Year's gifts of Queen Elizabeth the bodkin is often mentioned and usually described as of gold with a jewelled pendant. (See Nichols' *Progresses of Queen Elizabeth*.)  Baret, in his dictionary, says, " a bodkine or big needle to crest the heeres."

(*c*) Baret further says, " A bodkine or fine instrument that women curle their heire withall, it may be called friseling iron."

(*d*) An instrument used for puncturing holes in fabric.

BOLT.  A short thick arrow used with a cross-bow. See Bow.

BOMBASIN—BOMBAZINE.  " Stuffe that's made of cotton or of cotton and linnen." (Cotgrave, 1611.)

BOMBAST—BUMBAST.  Stuffiing for such garments as doublet and hose to make them stand out.
" Here comes lean Jack, here comes bare-bone—
How now, my sweet creature of bombast !  How Long is't ago, Jack, since thou sawest thine own knee ? "

(Shakespeare, 1st *Henry IV*—II. IV. 363)

(The word bombast is often used metaphorically.)

BONE-LACE.  Lace worked on a pillow with pins and bobbins, then called " bones."  See LACE.
" The spinsters and the knitters in the sun,
And the free maids that weave their thread with bones."

(Shakespeare, *Twelfth Night*—II. IV. 45.)

BON-GRACE.  A protection against the sun.  Although there are numerous allusions to this word, the exact form of a bon-grace is not clear.
" Bonne-grace, uppermost flap of the down hanging taile of a French-hood (whence like our Boongrace)."

(Cotgrave, 1611.)

Also, under " cornetta," Cotgrave says, " a fashion of shadow, or Boonegrace, used in old time, and at this day, by some old women."

BOOT.  High leather foot gear worn primarily for riding, but used also for walking.  They were sometimes folded down below the knee ready to be drawn up over the knee when so desired.

They were worn smooth or wrinkled, tight fitting or loose.  Sometimes the leather was slashed or punctured to assure a better fit.

Falstaff :  " [He] wears his boots very smooth, like unto the sign of the leg."

(Shakespeare, 2nd *Henry IV*—II. IV. 270.)

" When of a sudden, casting mine eyes lower, I beheld a curious pair of boots of King Philip's (Spanish) leather, in such artificial wrinkles, sets, and plaits, as if they had been starched lately and came new from the laundress's, such was my ignorance and simple acquaintance with the fashion, and I dare swear my fellows and neighbours here are all as ignorant as myself.  But that which struck us most into admiration : upon those fantastical boots stood such huge and wide tops, which so swallowed up his thighs, that had he sworn as other gallants did, this common oath, ' Would I might sink as I stand ! ' all his body might very well have sunk down and been damned in his boots." (Thomas Middleton's *Father Hubburd's Tales*, 1604.)

For Foot Gear in general, see SHOE.

BOOT HOSE.  " A thicke hose worne instead of a boot." (Cotgrave.)

" . . . with a linen stock on one leg and a kersey boot hose on the other . . . " (Shakespeare, *Taming of the Shrew*—III. II. 69).

One would infer from Stubbes (see page 44) that the boot hose was also a protective stocking worn inside the boot.

BORATTO.  A light stuff of silk and fine wool. (Fairholt.)

BORDERS.  Bands of trimming for garments.

BOW.  The bow was still carried in infantry warfare, though after 1600 it fell into disuse in favour of fire arms.  It continued to be used for sporting purposes such as hunting and archery.

(*a*) LONG Bow was made of one piece preferably yew and varying in length according to the height of the user, 5 ft. 6 in.—6 ft. 8 in.

(*b*) CROSS-BOW was a heavy T-shaped bow.  (See CROSS-BOW.)

(*c*) LATCH was another name for the cross-bow of the 16th century.

(*d*) PROD was a light cross-bow for shooting deer. Sometimes used by women.

The ARROW for a long bow was usually called a " SHAFT."  For the cross bow it was shorter and thicker and called a " BOLT."

BOWMAN.  See ARCHER.

BRACELET.  For this subject, consult the illustrations.

BREAST PLATE.  That part of armour which covered the breast.  It will be seen that the " peascod bellied " civilian fashion was carried out in the breast plate at this time. See illus. on page 93.

BREECHES. We shall treat the subject of men's loin and leg covering under this heading, although this garment was at first known under such names as the following : French Hose, Trunk Hose, Round Hose, Hose or Hosen, Venetians, Upper Stocks, Galley Hosen, Gally Gaskins, Slops, Breeches.

From Stubbes we have the following :—

" The French Hose are of two divers makings, for the common french-hose contayneth length, breadth, and sidenes sufficient, and is made very round. The other contayneth neither length, breadth nor sidenes (being not past a quarter of a yarde side), whereof some be paned, cut and drawne out with costly ornaments, with Canions annexed reaching down beneath their knees." See illus. on page 37.

The French Hose was known also as Round Hose or Trunk Hose. See illus. on page 21. To this type was annexed a pair of stockings, the two garments worn as one, being fastened together. They were alluded to as Upper Stocks and Nether Stocks. As the period advanced, they became separate articles.

Venetians. Again from Stubbes we have, " The Venetian hosen reach beneath the knee to the gartering place beneathe the knee." See illus. on page 36.

Gally Hosen or Gally-Gascoynes or Gaskins. Stubbes continues, " The gally-hosen are made very large and wide, reaching downe to their knees onely, with three or foure guardes apeece laid down along either hose."

Slops. As the name implies, any loose wide breeches. See illus. on page 34. The gally hosen were sometimes known as " slops." See under Slop.

There was in addition an uncommon form of breeches, open at the knee. See illus. on page 66. See also page 18.

BRIDE LACE. Ribbons or streamers worn by guests at a wedding.

" . . . all the lusty lads and bold bachelors of the parish, suitably every wight with his blue buckram bridelace upon a branch of green broom ('cause rosemary is scant there) tied on his left arm " (Laneham's account of a country wedding arranged for the amusement of Queen Elizabeth at Kenilworth, 1575.)

Laneham continues, " . . . the bride cup . . . adorned with a beautiful branch of broom . . . from which two broad bridelaces of red and yellow buckram begilded . . ." (Nichols' *Progresses of Queen Elizabeth*.)

" A nosegay bound with laces in his hat,
Bride-laces, Sir, and his hat all green."

(H. Porter, *Two Angry Women of Abington*, 1599.)

BRIGANDINE. A flexible military defence for the body. In outward appearance it was a close jacket often of velvet, studded with rivet heads. The canvas lining of this garment was completely reinforced by overlapping steel plates, held in place by rivets, the heads of which appeared on the surface, as stated above. Baret's dictionary says " Brigantine—or coate of fence double plated or double nailed."

BROCADE. Textile enriched on its surface with decorative weaving in low relief. Brocade was much used for the garments of both sexes.

BROOCH. An ornament usually jewelled and worn about the neck, or as a buckle, clasp or breast pin. Most particularly worn by both sexes as a hat or cap decoration. See illus. on page 66.

' Hat . . . tyed up before, and a brooch of copper, wherein Saint George sate verye well mounted."

(Robert Greene, *Greenes vision*, 1592.)

BUCKLER. A small shield used by swordsmen to ward a blow, made of metal or wood covered with leather and studded. It usually had a spike in the centre and a strap on the inner side to fit over the wrist or knuckles.

" Until the twelfe or thirteenth yeere of Queene Elizabeth, the auncient English fight of Sworde and Buckler was only had in use, the Bucklers then being but a foote broad, with a pike of 4 or 5 Inches long, then they beganne to make them full half ell broad, with sharpe pikes 10 or 12 Inches long, wherewith they meant eyther to breake the swords of their enemies, if it hitte upon the pike, or els sodainly to runne within them to stabbe and thrust their Buckler with the pike into the Face, arme, or Body of their adversary ; but this continued not long, every haberdasher then sold Bucklers." (Howes' edn. of Stow's *Annales*, 1615.)

" Take down my buckler and sweep the cobwebs off, and grind the pick on't and fetch a nail or two and tack on the bracers. Your mistress made a pot lid on't, I thank her, at her maids wedding and burnt off the handle." (Beaumont and Fletcher, *Cupid's Revenge*, 1612.)

BUCKLES. " . . . And about the time afore mentioned [1567-8] and many yeeres before, many honourable personages wore their shooes with buckles, viz. the common sort wore copper buckles, and the best sort wore buckles of silver, or copper gilded. But concerning shooe Roses . . . they were not then used." (Howes' edn. of Stow's *Annales*, 1615.) See Rose.

BUCKRAM. Coarse linen stiffened with gum.

" . . . two rogues in buckram suits."

(Shakespeare, 1st *Henry IV*.—II. IV. 217.)

BUDGE. Lambskin with the wool dressed outward. Used as trimming and lining. " I lighted upon an old straddling Usurer clad in . . . a short thrid bare gown on his backe, fac't with moath-eaten budge." (Nashe, *Pierce Penilesse*, 1592.)

BUFF COAT. A coat for soldiers' wear, made of stout leather, usually sleeveless.

" And is not a buffe jerkin a most sweet robe of durance." (Shakespeare, 1st *Henry IV*.—I. II. 48.) See illus. on page 91.

BUFFE. An arrangement of three or more horizontal lames affixed to that part of the burgonet which covered the face and chin. It could be raised and lowered. See Beaver.

BUFFIN. Coarse material used for gowns by the middle classes.

BUGLES. Glass beads much used as ornaments especially for women's hair.

On New Year's Day, 1579, Mrs. Wingfield gave Elizabeth " a chaine and a border of bewegels and seed perles very smale."— (Nichol's *Progresses of Queen Elizabeth*.)

BULLET BAG. A leather pouch, carried by musqueteers, which contained their bullets. See illustration on page 99.

BUREL—BURRELL. " Black burrell " is mentioned among the remnants of silk in Queen Elizabeth's wardrobe in 1600. A coarse woollen cloth. (*O.E.D.*)

BURGONET. An open-faced helmet with ridged crest, worn in war and in the tilt yard. For protection to the face, the buffe was often attached.

" A certaine kind of head peece, either for foote or horsemen, covering the head, and part of the face and cheeke." (Barret, *Theorike of Warres*, 1597-8.)

" Burgonets of good depth well lined and stuffed for the easiness of their heads and tied with a red scarfe under their chinnes and that they should not wear them flapping open untied." (Sir John Smythe, *Instructions*, written 1591.)

BUSK. A rigid piece of wood or whalebone set down the front of a corset or stomacher to give a straight effect to the body. " A buske, plated bodie, or other quilted thing worne to make or keep the body straight." (Cotgrave, *Dictionarie*, 1611.)

" The baudie buske that keepes downe flat
The bed wherein the babe should breed."

(Gosson, *Pleasant quippes*, 1595.)

Winifred : " Oh, I could crack my whalebones, breake my Buske, to think what laughter may arise from this." (Marston, *Jack Drum's entertainment*, 1601.)

BUSK POINT. The lacing and its tag or tip which secured the end of the busk.

BUSKINS. (a) A covering for the foot and leg reaching to the calf, or to the knee ; a half boot. (O.E.D.)

In describing the Bohemians, Moryson says, " and upon their legges they weare white buskins wrought with velvet at the toes." (Itinerary.) See page 14.

(b) A loose short stocking made of precious stuff or cloth of gold, enriched with ornamentation, and worn by pope and bishops.

BUSTIAN. A kind of coarse cloth. (Halliwell's Dic.)

BUTTONS. Among the illustrations may be seen many types of buttons. They were made of metal, or cloth covered, bone, jewels, horn, mother of pearl, ivory, jet, glass or wood, etc.

"The very best sort " began wearing buttons " of the same stuffe, their doublets, coats or Jerkins were made of." (Howes' edn. of Stow's Annales, 1615.)

"At which time likewise, many very honourable personages, and others, as well women as men, did weare borders of great Christall buttons about their cappes, or hatbands, as a worthy garment, to distinguish betweene the Gentry and others. But about the tenth yeere of Queene Elizabeth [1567-8] many young Citizens and others, began to weare Christall buttons upon their doublets, coats, and Jerkins, and then the former wearing of borders and hatbands, set with Christall buttons ceased. And within few yeeres after, began the generall wearing of buttons, of threed, silke, haire, and of gold and silver threed." (Stow, Annales, ed. 1631.)

CABASSET. A steel helmet with high rounded crown and a narrow brim, also called " Spanish morion."
See MORION. See illus. on page 97.

CADDIS—CADDICE. Wool or worsted, made into tape or binding or ribbon, sometimes called cruel or crewel.
" Caddis-garter " is mentioned by Shakespeare, 1st Henry IV—II. IV. 80.

CALICO. Cotton fabric at this time imported from India. " I can fit you, Gentlemen, with fine callicoes too for your dublets ; the onely sweet fashion now, most delicate and courtly : a meeke gentle callico, cut upon two double affable taffetaes, ah, most neate, feate and unmatchable ! " (Dekker, The honest whore, 1604.)

CALIMANCO. A glazed fabric.

CALIVER. A light kind of musket or harquebus fired without a " rest."

" His Caliver . . . must be in length at the least three foote and two ynches, and the bore must be in Diameter ¾ of a ynch." (Tartaglia, Colloq., 1588.)

" . . . such as fear the report of a caliver worse than a struck fowl or a hurt wild duck." (Shakespeare, 1st Henry IV—IV. II. 20.)

CAMBRIC—CAMERICKE. Fabric introduced at this period from Cambrai, France. Stubbes says, " The women . . . use great ruffes and neckerchers of holland, lawne, camerick, and such cloth, as the greatest thred shall not be so bigge as the least hair that is." (Anatomy of Abuses.) See STARCH. See LAWN.

CAMLET—CAMELOTT—CHAMLET—CAMELOT
" Mixture of silk and cashmere." (Quicherat.)
" Made of the hair of the angora goat." (Onions.)
" Mixed stuff of wool and silk." (Fairholt.)
" Originally manufactured of the hair of the camel." (Fairholt.)
Stubbes says, " . . . Their dublets be made, some of Saten, Taffatie, silk, Grogram, Chamlet, gold, silver, and what not." (Anatomy of Abuses.)
" I went to see their manufactures of silke, their pressing and watering the grograms and chambletts." (Evelyn's Diary, 1644.)
" Let me see that chamblet, is it watred or unwatred ?" (Erondell, French Garden, 1605.) See V. Gay, Glossaire Archéologique.

CANE. Although walking sticks were known at this period they were not yet in general use.

CANIONS. In describing the various fashions in men's breeches, under " French Hose," Stubbes says, " . . . whereof some be paned, cut and drawne out with costly ornaments, with Canions annexed reaching down beneath the knees." (Anatomy of Abuses.)

In studying contemporary portraits and following Stubbes' description it will be noted in many instances that men are wearing short trunks adjoining which are tubular continuations, or swathings of contrasting material, silk or velvet, plain, brocaded or embroidered. The stockings are tucked under, or rolled up over these canions. See illus. on page 30.

(His poignard) " . . . cut mee a payre of very imperiall cloth of golde hose, at least thus long thwart the cannon . . ." (Dekker, Patient Grissil, 1603.)

" Cannions of breeches, because they are like cannons of artillery, or cans or pots." (Minsheu, Guide unto Tongues, 1617.)

CANVAS. A material such as we know it to-day. Canvas doublets are mentioned by Shakespeare and by Dekker.

CAP. The CLOSE CAP, somewhat like a " baby cap " was worn by women and children, sometimes topped by a bonnet or a brimmed hat. The same type was often worn by elderly men made either of linen, lace, silk, brocade, or velvet.

Professional men, such as lawyers or doctors, also wore the close cap (See COIF, PILEUS.) The cap which Petruchio ridicules in Taming of the Shrew, probably barely covered the crown of the skull :
" Why, this was moulded on a porringer ;
A velvet dish : fie, fie ! 'tis lewd and filthy :
Why, 'tis a cockle or a walnut-shell—
A knack, a toy, a trick, a baby's cap :
Away with it ! come, let me have a bigger . . . "
He continues :
" . . . it is a paltry cap,
A custard-coffin, a bauble, a silken pie."
From Ben Jonson in Every Man in his Humour, 1601, we have :—
" Our great heads,
Within this city, never were in safety
Since our wives wore these little caps : I'll change
'em,
I'll change 'em straight in mine : mine shall no
more
Wear three-piled acorns, to make my horns ake."
" His Majesty came in Person into the Lords House of Parliament and being placed under the Estate in his Roabes, wearing his capp and Imperiall Crowne . . . "
(Parliamentary Diary of Robert Bowyer—1606-7 ; D. H. Willson.)
See illus. on page 52.

KNIT CAPS. Between the years 1568 and 1574 " All Citizens wives in generall, were constrayned to weare white knit Caps of woolen yarne, unlesse their husbands were of good value in the Queenes booke, or could prove themselves Gentlemen by descent." (Howe, 1631, Stow's Annales.)

MINEVOR CAPS. " . . . then ceased the womens wearing of Minevor caps, otherwise called three corner Caps which formerly was the usuall wearing of all grave Matrons. These Minevor Caps were white, and three square, and the peakes thereof were full three or foure inches from their head." (Ibid.)

FLAT CAPS. " They also wore flat Caps, both then and many yeares after, as well Apprentizes as Journey-men and others, both at home and abroad, whom the Pages of the Court in derision called ' Flat Caps.' " (Harrison, Description of England.)

STATUTE CAPS. Woollen caps ordered by an act of parliament of 1571 to be worn " upon the Saboth and Holy Daye " by " all and every person and persons above Thage of syxe yeres' except women and certain officials." (Onions, *Glossary*.)

"Nay, though my husband be a citizen and 's cap's made of wool, yet I h'wit . . ." (Marston's *Dutch Courtezan*, 1605.)

MONMOUTH CAP. I have found no description or contemporary illustration of the cap mentioned by Shakespeare as the "honourable badge of the service." In *The Song of the Caps*, a late Elizabethan ballad, further extracts of which are given below, there appears this line : "The souldiers that the Monmouth wear."

See Moryson's comments, page 17.

"The quilted, furr'd, the velvet, satin,
For which so many pates learn Latin :

\* \* \*

The crewell Cap, the fustian pate . . .

\* \* \*

The saylors with their thrums doe stand

\* \* \*

The sick mans Cap not wrought with silk,
Is like repentant, white as milk.
When hats in church drop off in haste,
This Cap ne'er leaves the head uncaste :
The sick mans Cap, if wrought, can tell
Though he be ill, his state is well.

\* \* \*

The furr'd and quilted Cap of age . . .

\* \* \*

The crewell Cap is knit like hose
For them whose zeale takes cold i' th' nose ;

\* \* \*

The Satin and the velvet hive
Unto a bishoprick doe drive . . ."
*The Song of the Caps*, (Roxburgh Ballads)

CAP-A-PIE ARMOUR. Complete armour, or from head to foot. See illus. on page 94.

CAPE. "Some have Capes reaching to the middest of their backs, faced with Velvet, or els with some fine wrought silk Taffatie at the least, and fringed about very bravely ; and (to shut up all in a word) some are pleated and created down the back wonderfully, with more knacks than I can declare." (Stubbes, *Anatomy*.)

CAPOUCH—CAPUCHE. A monk's cowl or hood, also the hood of a cloak. See HOOD.

CAPPA. See COPE.

CAPUTIUM. A hood, usually worn by scholars or ecclesiastics. See HOOD.

CARBINE—CARABEN—CARABIN. A rifle shorter than the musket, used mostly for mounted troops.

". . . shot-on-horsebacke, but now lately called carbines . . . these carbines may skyrmidge loosely, and delivering theyr volleies are not able to stand any charge, but must retire to the launce for his safety." (Barnabie Rich, *Pathway to military practice*, 1587.)

CARCANET—CARKENET—CARKANETTE. Gold or jewelled necklace, bracelet or hair ornament.

". . . one riche carkenet or collor of golde, haveing in it two emeraldes, 4 rubyes, and fully garnished with small rubyes and dyamondes. Given by the erle of Lecetor." New Year's Gift presented to Queen Elizabeth, 1573. (Nichols' *Progresses of Queen Elizabeth*.)

"Curled haires hung full of sparkling carkanets." (Marston's *Antonio and Mellida*, 1601.)

CARDINAL'S ATTIRE. The cardinal was, next to the Pope, the highest dignitary of the Roman Church. He wore a red hat or a biretta, a rochet and a mozetta. See CASSOCK.

See illus. on page 88.

CARNATION. "The hew or colour of one's skin and flesh." (Florio.)

"A' could never abide carnation ; 'twas a colour he never liked." (Shakespeare, *Henry V*—II. III. 35.)

CARRELLS. A mixed fabric of silk and worsted. (Fairholt.)

CARRIAGES. An arrangement of straps hanging from the girdle and holding the sword. According to Shakespeare, carriages and hangers would appear to be synonymous :

Osric : ". . . six French rapiers, and poniards, with their assigns, as girdle, hangers and so : three of the carriages, in faith, are very dear to fancy, very responsive to the hilts, most delicate carriages, and of very liberal conceit."

Hamlet : "What call you the carriages ?"

Osric : "The carriages, Sir, are the hangers."
(Shakespeare, *Hamlet*—V. II. 157.)

CARSEY. See KERSEY.

CASQUE. General term for the military head piece or helmet.

Gaunt : "And let thy blows, doubly redoubled,
Fall like amazing thunder on the casque
Of thy adverse pernicious enemy : "
(Shakespeare, *Richard II*—I. III. 81.)

CASSOCK. A loose outward coat.

"A grave man in a black velvet cassock, like a counsellor." (Lingua, 1607.)

". . . an old straddling Usurer, clad in a damaske cassocke, edged with Fox-fur." (Nashe's *Pierce Penilesse*, 1592.)

". . . shake the snow from off their cassocks . . ." (the allusion is to soldiers' coats). (Shakespeare, *All's Well*—IV. III. 193.)

". . . that the bayliffs and aldermen, in the receipt of her Majestie, shall ride upon comely geldings with foot-clothes in damask or sattin cassocks or coats . . . The councell to attend upon the bayliffs and aldermen . . . in grogram or silk cassock coate or jackets . . ." (Nichols' *Progresses of Queen Elizabeth*.)

(2) Distinctive outer garment of the clergy on ordinary occasions. It was worn under the alb, hence scarcely visible for Eucharistic office. For processional attire it showed under the surplice. Because its purpose was for warmth it was lined with fur. The cassock was black for ordinary ecclesiastics, scarlet for doctors of divinity and cardinals, purple for bishops and prelates and on high occasions for acolytes, for the Pope, white. Ermine fur was used for dignitaries, sheepskin for priests. (Macalister's *Ecclesiastical Vestments*, 1896.)

CASTING BOTTLE. Bottle for sprinkling perfume. See allusion under MIRROR.

CAUL—CAWLE. Close-fitting cap usually of net.

"These glittering cawles of golden plate,
Wherewith their heads are richlie dect."
(Gosson's *Pleasant quippes*, 1595-6.)

". . . cawles, made Netwyse to th'ende . . . that the clothe of gold, cloth of silver or els tinsell . . . wherewith their heads are covered . . . underneath their cawles maye appeare, and shewe it selfe in the bravest maner. Soe that a man that seethe them . . . wold thinke them to have golden heads." (Stubbes' *Anatomy of Abuses*.)

See also HAIR DRESSING.

CAVALRY. "Cavalry hath been divided into foure kinds, the first men at armes, themselves, armed complet, and theyr horses likewise barded, and were to give the first charge, to discover the squadrons or battalions of pikes. The second launces, lighter armed with corselets . . . The third light horsemen, commonly armed with a coat of plate, with a light staffe charged on the theigh . . . The fourth and last called shot-on-horsebacke, but now lately called Carbines . . ."
(Barnabie Rich's *Pathway to military practice*, 1587.)

CHAINS. As costume accessory chains may be studied throughout the illustrations.

Chains were, as badge of office, worn by mayors, aldermen, gentlemen ushers, stewards :—

"By this staff of office that commands you,
This chain and double ruff, symbols of power . . ."

(Steward addressing the Servants in Massinger's *New way to pay old debts*, 1632-3.)

"Go, sir, rub your chain with crumbs."

(Sir Toby Belch to Malvolio, steward, in Shakespeare's *Twelfth Night*—II. III. 130.)

"The Queen presents every mayor at his election with a chain." (Von Wedel's *Letters*—1585, Ed. Klarwill.)

CHAMLET. See CAMLET.

CHAPERON. "A hood or French hood (for a woman) ; also any hood, bonnet or lattice cap." (Cotgrave.)

"The women [of France] have an attire more modest [than the men] and less changeable. The noble woman wears on her head a chaperon of black velvet . . . she has a mask over her face. The women of the bourgeosie wear a chaperon of cloth, because the silk coiffure and the mask is forbidden them." (V. Gay, *Glossaire*.)

See HOOD.

CHAPINEY. See CHOPINE.

CHASUBLE (Also called VESTMENT). The outermost mass vestment, whose general form at this period was an elongated oval with a hole in the centre for the head. It was made of silk or other precious stuff such as velvet, brocade, cloth of gold. In Cotgrave's dictionary it is described : "A chasuble, a fashion of cope thats open onely in the sides ; and is worne at Masse both by the Priest (who hath it round) and his assistant Deacon, and Subdeacon, who have it square, in the bottom." (1611.)

CHEVERIL. Kid leather, noted for its flexibility.

CHIMERE. A long sleeveless ecclesiastical gown of black satin or silk, open down the front. The lawn sleeves of the rochet, worn underneath, were set into the armholes. It was worn in this form by post-reformation ecclesiastics.

See illus. on page 90.

CHIN CLOTH. "Mantonniere—a chinne-cloth or a little peece of fine linnen wherewith a masked Ladie covers her chinne." (Cotgrave, 1611.)

CHOIR VESTMENTS. "The gentlemen and children in their surplices, and the priests in copes." (Heylyn's *History of the Reformation*, 1661.)

CHOPINE—CHAPINEY. "A kind of high slippers for low women." (Cotgrave.) They were worn in Spain and in Italy, especially Venice.

". . . Your Ladyship is nearer heaven than when I saw you last, by the altitude of a chopine."

(Shakespeare, *Hamlet*—II. II. 455.)

Coryat in his *Crudities*, in speaking of the chopine as he observed it says " (it is) so common in Venice, that no woman whatsoever goeth without it, either in her house or abroad ; a thing made of wood, and covered with leather of sundry colours, some with white, some redde, some yellow. It is called a ' Chapiney,' which they weare under their shoes. Many of them are curiously painted, some also I have seen fairely gilt . . . Also I have heard that this is observed amongst them, that by how much the nobler a woman is, by so much the higher are her Chapineys. All the Gentlewomen, and most of the wives and widowes that are of any wealth, are assisted and supported eyther by men or women when they walk abroad, to the end they may not fall . . . For I saw a woman fall a very dangerous fall, as she was going downe the staires of one of the stony bridges with her high Chapineys, alone by her selfe ; but I did nothing pity her, because shee wore such frivolous and (as I may truly term them) ridiculous instruments, which were the occasion of her fall."

In France they were called PATTENS. (See that word.)

See Villamont's account page 19.

CLOAK. "Cloakes . . . of dyverse and sundry colours, white, red, tawnie, black, greene, yellowe, russet, purple, violet and infynite other colours : some of cloth, silk, velvet, taffetie, and such like, whereof some be of the Spanish, French, and Dutch fashion : some short, scarsely reaching to the gyrdle-stead, or wast, some to the knee, and othersome traylinge upon the ground (almost) liker gownes than clokes. These clokes must be garded, laced, and thorowly faced ; and sometimes so lyned as the inner side standeth almost in as much as the outside : some have sleeves, othersome have none ; some have hoodes to pull over the head, some have none ; some are hanged with points and tassels of gold, silver, or silk, some without al this." (Stubbes.)

"Here is a cloke cost fifty pound, wife.
Which I can sell for thirty, when I have seen
All London in't and London has seen me."

(Ben Jonson, *The Devil is an ass*, 1616)

"Because we walke in Jerkins and in Hose
Without an upper Garment, Cloake or Gowne
We must be Tapsters running up and downe
With Cannes of Beere . . ."

(S. Rowlands' *The knave of harts*, 1612.)

CLOCK. "Clocks about the ancles." (Stubbes.) A decoration or a gore, as may be seen illustrated on page 77.

CLOG. A crude wooden soled shoe or sandal worn chiefly by women in some localities to protect the feet from wet. It was also a sole of wood or leather worn under the shoe as a protection and was attached to the shoe by straps or ties.

CLOUT. A piece of coarse cloth, a rag.

COAT. Upper garment, a gown, a jacket.

COCKLE HAT. A hat with a scallop-shell stuck in it, worn by pilgrims as a sign of their having been to the shrine of St. James of Compostella in Spain. (Onions, *Glossary*.)

CODPIECE. An artificial protuberance to the breeches (Halliwell's *Dictionary*.)

See Moryson on page 15.

COGWARE. A coarse kind of cloth, apparently resembling frieze, made of the most inferior wool. (*O.E.D.*)

COIF. The coif of the Serjeant-at-Law, which was the highest order of council at the English bar, is illustrated on page 82.

It was made of white silk or lawn, and usually tied under the chin with strings. When not engaged in a cause, the serjeant and the judges wore upon the white coif, a silk or velvet cap of the same shape, but slightly smaller showing the edge of the white coif beneath.

See CAP.

COLLAR. ". . . The collar of it [the doublet] rose up so high and sharp as if it would have cut his throat by daylight." (T. Middleton's *The ant and the nightingale*, 1604.)

"Let us have standing Collers in the fashion." (S. Rowlands' *The knave of harts*, 1612.) See BAND.

Collar of the orders of Knighthood. See KNIGHTHOOD.

COMB. The following is an extract from Peter Erondell's *The French Garden* : ". . . go too, I am combed enough. Page take the combe-brushes, and make cleane my combes, take heed you doe not make them cleane with those that I use to my head : take a quill and take away the filth to them, and then put them in the case, that none be missing : go too, make an end of dressing my head."

COPATAIN—COPITANK. Hat with a high conical crown. Also called " steeple " or " sugar-loaf."

Vin.: "What am I, Sir ! nay, what are you, Sir ? O immortal gods ! O fine villain ! A silken doublet ! a velvet hose ! a scarlet cloak ! and a copatain hat ! O, I am undone ! while I play the good husband at home, my son and my servant spend all at the university." (Shakespeare, *Taming of the Shrew*—V. I. 66.)

COPE. Liturgical vestment worn by both Catholic and Protestant church. An almost semi-circular cape " worn in processions, at vespers, during celebration of mass by some of assistant clergy, at benedictions, consecrations and other ecclesiastical functions." (Pugin, *Glossary*.) It was fastened in front by a brooch, called a morse. At the neck was attached a hood or a shield-shaped piece of material hanging over the back.

" The Queenes Maiesties most royall proceeding in State from Somerset place to Pauls church, 1588 . . . the Bishop of London in his Cope, delivered her a book . . . in the presence of all the Prebends and Churchmen, who attended her Highnesse in very rich Copes." (W. Segar, *Honor, military and civil*, 1602.)

CORDOVAN. Spanish leather.

CORDUROY. A thick durable ribbed or corded material.

CORKED SHOES. Between the foot and the sole was a wedge of cork usually rising toward the heel.
Cork-soled shoes, see page 76.

CORONATION ROBE. See ROBE.

CORONET. Crown of the nobility. See Burke's *Peerage.*

CORSET. The usual terms for the corset at this time were : " privie-coate," " whale-bone bodies " or " petty-coate bodyes with whale-bones."
" These privie coates, by art made strong
With bones, with past, and such like ware,
Whereby their backe and sides grow long,
And now they harnest galants are ;
Were they for use against the foe'
Our dames for Amazons might go."
(Gosson, *Pleasant quippes.*)
" He'll have an attractive Lace
And whalebone bodyes, for a better grace."
(Henry Fitzgeffrey, *Notes from Black Fryers*, 1617.)
" Bring my petty-coate bodies, I mean my damask quilt bodies with whale bones, what lace doe you give me heere ? this lace is too shorte, the tagges are broken, I cannot lace myselfe with it." (Erondell's, *The French Garden*, 1605.)

CORSLET. A suit of half armour.
" . . . And such as are appointed to have corslettes furnished, that is, to have good curates for their bodies, taces for their thighes, poldrones and vambraces for their shoulders and arms, burgonites for their heads." (Thomas Styward, *Pathwaie to Martiall Discipline*, 1581.)
See what Sir Roger Williams says under HALBARD.

COSMETICS.
" Where's the Devill ?
He's got into a boxe of Woman's paint . . .
Where pride is, thers the Devill too."
(*Quips upon Questions*, 1600.)
" The women, many of them, use to colour their faces with certain oyles, liquors, unguents and waters made to that end, whereby they think their beautie is greatly decored." (Stubbes.)
" Whosoever doo colour their faces, or their haire, with any unnaturall collour, they begin to prognosticate of which colour they shall be in hel." (*Ibid.*)
" . . . So steept in lemons juyce, so surphuled
I cannot see her face : "
(Jn. Marston, *Scourge of villainy*, 1598.)
" Handsome I cannot say any one of them was, but painted more (if it were possible) than the ordinary woman, not one of them free from it, though some of them not thirteen yeare old." (Notes by Sir Richard Wynne at Madrid. Nichols' *Progresses of James I.*)
" . . . I dare not say they are all harlots that paint, yet I may safely say, they have the harlot's badge, and their chastity is questionable." (T. Hall—1654.)
" . . . The ruddiness upon her lip is wet :
You'll mar it if you kiss it ; stain your own
With oily painting . . . "
(Shakespeare, *Winter's Tale*—V. III. 81.)

COVENTRY BLUE. " I have heard say that the chiefe trade of Coventry was heretofor in making blew threde, and then the towne was riche even upon that trade . . ." (William Stafford, 1581, *Fairholt.*)

COWL. A monk's hood. See MONASTIC ORDERS, CUCULLA, CAPOUCH.

CRESPINE—CRISPINE. At an earlier date this was a cap of net for binding up the hair. It was probably similar to the caul.
" V creppins of lawne garnesshed with golde and silver purle " were given to Queen Elizabeth on New Year's Day by Lady Ratcliffe, 1578. (Nichols' *Progresses of Queen Elizabeth.*)

CREWEL—CRUELL. Worsted. Garters are often mentioned as being made of crewel.
" His crewel garters cross about the knee."
(H. Porter, *Two angry women of Abington*, 1599.)

CROSIER—CROZIER also called PASTORAL STAFF. A crook-headed staff borne by bishop and archbishop and sometimes abbots as emblem of jurisdiction. " Archbishops are distinguished from bishops by having a staff with a cross or crucifix in its head, borne before them in addition. The prelate never bore the cross himself, except on the occasion of his investiture. He then received the cross into his own hands, but immediately passed it on to his cross-bearer." (Macalister's *Ecclesiastical Vestments.*)
In addition to the crosier and the cross staff, Pugin lists the following : —
Cantors' staff to regulate the chaunt and ceremonies of the choir. Processional staff for keeping order of procession. Staff used by confraternities, for carrying images and emblems. Staff of Honour and Office, called Verges or Maces, borne before dignitaries.
See illus. on pages 85 and 86.

CROSS. Pectoral cross was worn by bishops suspended around the neck by a chain and hanging on the breast.

CROSS-BOW. As a military weapon the cross-bow had long since been obsolete. As a sporting weapon, the cross-bow, sometimes called LATCH, was in popular use. A light kind of cross-bow much used by women for gaming was called a PRODD. The cross-bow was a " missile throwing weapon consisting of a bow fixed transversally upon a stock that contained a groove to guide the missile, a notch to hold the string of the bow, and a trigger to release it." (*Encyclopædia Britannica.*) They were usually fired with blunt-headed bolts. The STONE-BOW was a Cross-Bow which shot small stones instead of a bolt.
" O ! for a stone-bow, to hit him in the eye ! "
(Sir Toby in Shakespeare's *Twelfth Night*—II. V. 52.)

CROSS-CLOTH. A band of material bound across the forehead. Usually worn in connection with the coif. It was also used by women while ill in bed, and as a wrinkle preventative. Synonymous with or closely allied to cross-cloth were the words FOREHEAD-CLOTH, BINDING-CLOTH and FRONTLET, all of which are treated under this heading.
" When shall I have my binding cloath for my forehead ? Shall I have no . . . fore-head cloath ? " (Erondell's *French Garden.*)
" To cause them to sleepe . . . it is good to make a frontlet with the seede of poppie." (Surflet, " *Country Farm.*")
See FRONTLET, NIGHTCAP.

CROSS-GARTERING. " Hose garters going acrosse or overthwart, both above and beneath the knee." (Higins, *Junius' Nomenclator.*)
Garters made of ribbon or tape are cross gartered, when they are wound immediately below the knee, twisted behind the knee, and tied above the knee.
Malvolio : " . . . this does make some obstruction in the blood, this cross-gartering ; but what of that ? " (Shakespeare, *Twelfth Night*—III. IV. 23.)
See illus. on page 34.

CROWN. See crown of Queen Elizabeth on page 58.
See crown of James I on page 67.
See crown of Henry IV of France on page 84.

CUCULLA. A cowl or hood worn by Monks.
See MONASTIC ORDERS.

CUERPO—QUERPO. Informal attire for men, i.e., without cloak or gown.

See allusion to cuerpo under CLOAK.

CUFF. The cuff was an essential costume accessory and may be seen in its various forms in practically every contemporary portrait.

CUIRASS. A breast plate and a back plate of steel.

CUISSES—CUISH. Armour for the protection of the front part of the thigh. "His cushes on his thighs, gallantly arm'd." (Shakespeare, 1st *Henry IV*—IV. I. 105.)

"If he [Sir Philip Sidney] had that day worne his cuisses, the bullet had not broken his thigh bone . . ." (Sir John Smythe, *Certain Discourses*, 1590.)

CUTLASS — COUTELAS — CURTLE-AXE. Short broad cutting sword, with flat wide slightly curved blade, more for cutting than for thrusting.

CUT-WORK. See LACE.

CYPRESS—CYPRUS. A light transparent material resembling cobweb lawn or crepe, and like the latter it was, when black, much used for habiliments of mourning. See illus. on page 78.

" . . . him that weares the trebled cipers about his hatte . . ." (Dekker's *Guls horne-booke*, 1609.)

DAG. "A little pistoll." (Cotgrave.)

"Whilste he would show me how to hold the Dagge
To drawe the Cock, to charge and set the flint."
(Marston, *Jack Drum's entertainment*, 1601.)

DAGGER. "Seldom shall you see anie of my countriemen above eighteene or twentie yeeres old, go without a dagger, at the least, at his backe or by his side . . ."
(Harrison, *Description of England*, 1577.)

See illus. on page 36.

See allusion under SWORD.

DALMATIC. Mass vestment usually of costly fabric, and with wide sleeves. It was worn by bishops under the chasuble, and by deacons as the uppermost garment. See illus. on page 86.

DAMASK. A rich silk fabric woven with designs or figures. Also a twilled linen fabric.

" . . . table cloth and napkins of damaske."
(Erondell, *French Garden*, 1605.)

DEACON'S ATTIRE. Amice, alb, stole (worn over left shoulder), maniple and dalmatic. The deacon was next in dignity to the priest, who served as assistant to sacerdotal order, and whose duties were :—

(1) to sing the gospel in the mass and prepare the chalice, (2) to preach with the license of the bishop, (3) to baptise in absence of the priest, (4) to be almoner of the church, (5) to assist bishops in council, (6) to distribute the Holy Eucharist, or only the chalice. (Pugin.)

See page 87.

The SUB DEACON. First of the Holy Orders whose office it was to wash the altar cloth, corporals, and the mundatories, to give the chalice and paten to the deacon at offertory, to pour water into the chalice, and generally to minister to the deacon in mass, to sing the epistle. He wore the tunicle over a girded alb, with maniple. (*Ibid.*)

See illus. on page 87.

DIRK. A dagger.

DOUBLET. Close-fitting upper body-garment, worn next to the shirt, terminating at the waist or below. Worn by men and sometimes by women. Sleeves accompanied the doublet but were often detachable, fastening at the armhole, by means of points or even pins.

" . . . their Dublets be made, some of Saten, Taffatie, silk Grogram, Chamlet, gold, silver, and what not ; slashed, jagged, cut, carved, pincked and laced with all kinde of costly lace of divers and sundry colours." (Stubbes, *Anatomy of Abuses*.)

"The Women also have dublets and Jerkins . . . buttoned up the breast, and made with wings, welts,

and pinions on the shoulder points, as mans apparel is for all the world . . ." (Stubbes, *Anatomy*.) See illus. on page 25.

For " peascod-bellied " doublet, see illus. on pages 37 and 45.

See BOMBAST.

DOWLAS. Coarse kind of linen imported from Brittany and worn chiefly by the lower classes. (Hal.)

Hostess : " I bought you a dozen of shirts to your back."

Falstaff : " Dowlas, filthy dowlas : I have given them away to bakers' wives, and they have made bolters of them." (Shakespeare, 1st *Henry IV*—III. III. 77.)

DRESS. See GOWN.

DURANCE—DURITY. Durable fabric.

EAR PICK. " An earpicke of gold enamuled, garnished with sparcks of rubyes, blue saphires and seede perle." (Presented to Queen Elizabeth, 1575. Nichols' *Progresses of Queen Elizabeth*.)

EARRINGS. Both men and women wore earrings, as may be seen by contemporary portraits. See illustrations.

EAR STRING. A black string drawn through a hole in the left ear, and hanging sometimes to the shoulder. An eccentricity appearing toward the latter part of the period. See illus. page 73.

See SHOE STRINGS.

ECCLESIASTICAL VESTMENTS. See VESTMENT.

EMBROIDERY. Needlework was much used at this period upon clothing, gloves and upon under garments. Shirts were commonly done in black or blue embroidery.

FABRIC. A list of fabrics is here given, the descriptions of which may be seen under their separate headings.

| | | | |
|---|---|---|---|
| anapes | carrells | lawn | sarcenet |
| armazine | cogware | linen | satin |
| baudekin | corduroy | linsey- | say |
| bays | cypress | woolsey | sendal |
| bombasin | damask | lockram | shag |
| boratto | dowlas | mockado | silk |
| brocade | durance | motley | stammel |
| buckram | felt | penistones | tabbinet |
| buffin | flannel | perpetuana | tabby |
| burel | frieze | plommettes | taffeta |
| bustian | fustian | plush | thrum |
| calico | gauze | puke | tiffany |
| calimanco | grogram | rash | tuft-taffeta |
| cambric | holland | rug | vandelas |
| camlet | kendal green | russet | velvet |
| canvas | kersey | | |

FALCHION. A sword with a curved edge, the edge being on the convex side.

" . . . saw thy murderous falchion smoking in his blood." (Shakespeare, *Richard III.*—I. II. 94.)

FALL, or Falling Band. A collar which falls or tends to fall upon the shoulders. The accompanying extracts together with the illustrations will best explain its variety of form.

" . . . you must wear falling bands ; you must come into the falling fashion : there is such a deal o' pinning these ruffs, when a fine cleane fall is worth all. . . . and again if you should chance to take a nap in the afternoon, your falling band requires no poking-stick to recover his form." (Marston's *Malcontent*, 1604.)

" . . . five yards of Lawne . . . to make . . . falling bands of the fashion, three falling one upon another, for that's the new edition now." (Dekker, *Honest whore*, 1604.)

" There she sat with her poking stick stiffening a fall." (*Laugh and Lie Down, or The World's Folly*, 1605.)

See Moryson on French attire, page 16 ; and on Italian attire on page 17.

FAN. Fans in great variety were commonly carried by women, as may be seen by many of the illustrations.

"Were fannes and flappes of feathers fond,
To flit away the flisking flies, . . . .
The wit of women we might praise, . . . .

But seeing they are stil in hand,
In house, in field, in church, in street,
In summer, winter, water, land,
In cold, in heate, in drie, in weet,
I judge they are for wives such tooles,
As bables are in plays for fooles."
(Gosson, *Pleasant quippes*, 1595.)

**FANON.** " Fanon, a fannell or maniple, a scarfe-like ornament worn in the left arm of a sacrificing priest." (Cotgrave.)

**FARTHINGALE — VERDUGARDE—VERDINGALE —VARDINGALE.** An under-contrivance designed to distend in circumference a woman's outer skirt. The earliest or Spanish type was " funnel " shaped, as may be seen in illus. on page 50.

The " Bolster " type is described in Cotgrave's dictionary as follows :—" Hausse-cul, a French Vardingale ; or (more properly) the kind of roll used by women, as weare no Vardingales." (1611.) See illus. on page 62.

Some were distended at the back and sides and almost flat in front.

Falstaff : " . . . and the firm fixture of thy foot would give an excellent motion to thy gait in a semi-circled farthingale." (Shakespeare, *Merry Wives*—III. III. 67.)

" A bombe lyke a barrell, with whoopes at the skyrte." (Robert Crowley's *Epigram of Nice Rogues*, 1550.)

" Whalebone wheeles." (Fitzgeffrey's *Satyres*, 1617.)
See Moryson's account under GERMANY on page 14.

**FEATHERS.** " And point the Feather-maker not to faile,
To plume my head with his best Estridge tayle."
(Rowlands' *A pair of spy-knaves*, 1619.)

" A fanne of sundry collored fethers with a handle of aggets garnished with silver gilte." New Year's Gift to Queen Elizabeth. (Nichols' *Progresses of Queen Elizabeth*, 1788-9.)

" . . . and many of them wore strange fethers of rich and great esteem, which they called ' The Birdes of Paradice.' " (Nichols' *Progresses of King James I ;* Entertainment of the King of Denmark, 1606.)

" His head was dressed up in white feathers like a shuttle-cock, which agreed so well with his brain, being nothing but cork, that two of the biggest of the guard might very easily have tossed him with battledores, and made good sport with him in his Majesty's great hall." (Thomas Middleton's *Father Hubburd's tales*, 1604.)

**FELT.** A fabric made of the fibre of furs and wool. It was largely used for hats toward the latter part of our period.

Lodo : " Mine is as tall a felt as any is this day in Millan, and therefore I love it, for the blocke was cleft out for my head, and fits me to a haire." (Dekker, *Honest whore*, 1604.)

**FLANNEL.** " Give me my waistecoate.
Which will you have, that of flannel ? "
(Florio, *Second Fruits*, 1591.)

**FOOL'S CAP.** " Chaperon de fou—a fooles cap set out with hornes, eares, ill faces, and other such fopperies." (Cotgrave, 1611.)
See MORRIS DANCER'S ATTIRE, MOTLEY.

**FOOT WEAR.** See SHOE.

**FOREHEAD CLOTH.** See CROSS-CLOTH.

**FOREPART.** A decorative piece of material inserted in the front of a woman's garment. In the wardrobe accounts of Queen Elizabeth, frequent mention is made of the forepart : " Forepart of a doublet " ; " Forepart of a kirtle."

In almost every item the forepart is made of precious material and elaborately embroidered.

**FRENCH HOOD.** See HOOD, HAT, CHAPERON.

**FRIEZE—FRIZE.** A coarse woollen cloth with a shaggy nap on one side. (*Standard Dictionary*.) Baret in 1580 said : " Frize—a rough garment that souldiers used, a mantle to cast on a bed, a carpet to laie on a table."

" Than which none warmer to be worn in winter, and the finest sort thereof very fashionable and genteele." (Fuller's *Worthies*, as quoted by Fairholt.)

" The Queen loveth to see me in my laste frize jerkin, and saithe 'tis well enough cutt. I will have another made like it." (Sir John Harington.)

**FRINGE.** " Give me my peticoate of wroughte Crimson velvet with silver fringe." (Erondell's *French Garden*, 1605.)

**FRISLET.** A kind of small ruffle. (*O.E.D.*)

**FRONTLET.** Forehead band. " Frontale—a frontlet, a fore-head piece. Also a square as women weare on their heads being sicke. Also a rowler to put on childrens heads to keepe them from hurt in falling." (Florio, 1611.)
See CROSS-CLOTH.

**FUR.** Fur was used for almost as many purposes as to-day, particularly as lining and edging to garments.

The skin of the whole animal is seen worn about the neck on page 23.

" The names of those beasts bearing furr, and now in use with the bountifull Society of Skinners :

" Ermine, foine, sables, martin, badger, bearre,
Luzernne, budge, otter, hipponesse, and hare,
Lamb, wolf, fox, leopard, minck, stot, miniver,
Racoon, moashy, wolverin, caliber,
Squirrel, mole, cat, musk, civet, wild and tame,
Cony, white, yellow, black, must have a name,
The ounce, rows gray, ginnell, pampilion,
Of birds the vulture, bitter, estridge, swan :
Some worn for ornament, and some for health,
All to the Skinners' art bring fame and wealth."
(T. Middleton, *Triumphs of love and antiquity*, 1619.)

**FUSTIAN.** Coarse cloth made of cotton and flax. (Onions, *Glossary*.)

" . . . and her hair trust up in a coife of fustian." (Innkeeper's daughter in night attire. Cervantes' *Don Quixote*, tr. Shelton, 1612)

" The serving men in their new fustian." (Shakespeare, *Taming of the Shrew*—IV. I. 49.)

**FUSTIAN ANAPES.** " Mocke-velvuet." (Cotgrave, 1632.)

**GABERDINE—GABARDINE.** Cotgrave in his dictionary (1611) calls : " Gaban,—a cloake of Felt, for raynie weather, a Gabardine." A loose upper garment. Neither Coryat nor Vecellio in their accounts of attire in Italy make any mention of " Jewish gaberdine," although both describe a hat peculiar to Jews.

" Alas ! the storm is come again : my best way is to creep under his gaberdine." (Shakespeare, *Tempest*—II. II. 41.)

**GALLY - GASCOYNES — GALLY - GASCOINE BREECHES — GALLY HOSEN — GASKINS.** Breeches. " The Gally-hosen are made very large and wide, reaching downe to their knees onely, with three or foure guardes a peece laid down along either hose." (Stubbes.)

Clo. : " . . . I am resolved on two points." See POINTS.

Mar. : " That if one break, the other will hold ; or, if both break, your gaskins fall." (Shakespeare, *Twelfth Night*—I. V. 27.)

**GALOCHE—GALAGE.** A protective overshoe, clog or patten. Its form is varied judging from the evidence at hand. Elyot (1538) says it " has nothing on the feet but only latchets." Cotgrave (1611) calls it " a woodden shooe or patten made all of a pieece, without any latchet or ty of leather, and worne by the poore clowne in Winter." According to Randal Holme (1688), " Galotia, a kind of false shooe, or a case for a shooe, to keep them clean in foul weather."

GAMACHE. High boots, buskins or startups. (Randal Holme, 1688.)

Quicherat says they were long buttoned gaiters which one placed over the stockings, some in velvet richly embroidered in gold and silver.

". . . a paire of Breeches and gamashoes of the same coloured cloth. His gamachoes were lifted up halfe the legge." (Cervantes, *Don Quixote*, tr. Shelton, 1612.)

GARDE. See GUARD.

GARTER. Garters were worn by both men and women above or below the knee. Men's garters grew into elaborate wide sash-like ties wound below the knee. See illus. on page 73.

See CROSS-GARTERING.

GASKINS. See GALLY GASCOYNES.

GAUNTLET. See GLOVE.

GAUZE. A thin transparent fabric of silk, linen or cotton. Many of the wired veils were made of gauze, net, tiffany or sarcenet.

GIRDLE. Girdles were worn by both men and women, and may be seen in their various forms among the illustrations.

GLAIVE—GLEAVE. A weapon consisting of a long cutting blade at the end of a lance. (Hal.)

GLOVE. By a study of the illustrations it will be seen that although the short glove was worn, the gauntlet type seems to have been popular. That gloves were often perfumed may be seen by the following :

"Their hands are covered with their sweet washed gloves, imbrodered with gold, silver, and what not." (Stubbes, *Anatomy of Abuses*.)

"Take your perfumed gloves that are lyned." (Erondell, *French Garden*.)

"Gloves as sweet as damask roses." (Shakespeare, *Winter's Tale*—IV. III. 222.)

Gloves were worn in hats as the favour of a mistress :—
"I have fine perfumed gloves
Made of the best doeskin :
Such as young men do give their loves
When they their favour win."

(D'Urfey, *Wit and Mirth*.)

They were worn as a mark to be challenged by an enemy :—

King Henry : "Soldier, why wear'st thou that glove in thy cap ? "

Williams : "An't please your majesty, 'tis the gage of one that I should fight withal . . ." (Shakespeare, *Henry V.*—IV. VII. 126.)

The illus. on page 95 will show that gloves might be worn in the hat as a memorial.

They served also the purpose of wedding favours :
"A glover sould two doozen of two peny gloves, which she gave to her friends." [At her wedding.]

(Robert Greene, *Greene's vision*, 1592.)

See allusion under PERFUME, under RING and ARCHER.

The Episcopal Glove of netted silk or other delicate material worn by bishop, archbishop, cardinal or pope, among the other mass vestments. Jewels were set into these gloves.

See MONIAL. See also illus. on page 85.

GORGET. (a) A military defence for the neck. This was one of the last portions of steel armour to be discarded, when armour gradually fell into disuse. See illus. on page 94.

(b) The gorget as woman's attire is described in an anonymous dictionary of 1571 : "A gorget, a Lawne wherewith women cover their pappes."

"And gorgets brave, with drawn-work wrought,
A tempting ware they are you know,
Wherewith (as nets) vaine youths are caught."

(Gosson, *Pleasant quippes*.)

GOWN. For men the gown was a loose outer garment, short, or more usually long. It was worn by officials, professional men, scholars and sedate and elderly men of all classes. The gowns were with or without sleeves, or with vertical slits for the arms.

"Every member (of Parliament) when he goes to the house or when many of his compeers are sitting in council, wears a peculiar old fashioned gown which reaches down to the ground." (Van Buchenbach, 1595, as quoted by Klarwill.)

In the thirtieth year of Elizabeth it was decreed that, "If any fellow of this House (Lincoln's Inn) . . . go abroad to London or Westminster without a gown, he should be put out of the Commons . . ." Also in the thirty-eighth of Elizabeth, "That what gentleman soever should come into the Hall at meal-time with any other upper garment then a gown, he should be suspended from being a member of the Society." (Dugdale's *Origines Juridiciales*, 1671.)

See Moryson's frequent mention of gowns for men, particularly the Venetians. (Page 17.)

The topmost dress of a woman was called " gown.' It might be a gown fastened up the front showing no part open, or an open gown revealing the " upper bodies," or the doublet, or the kirtle, or both.

". . . and as these gownes be of divers and sundrie colours, so are they of divers fashions, changing with the Moon . . . some with sleeves hanging down to their skirts, trayling on the ground, and cast over their shoulders, like Cowtayles." (Stubbes, *Anatomy of Abuses*.)

In the wardrobe accounts of Queen Elizabeth are described round gowns (closed), French gowns (open) and loose gowns (probably ungirded and flowing).

See CASSOCK. See ROCHET.

GREAVES. Armour protecting the lower leg. See illus. on page 94.

GREMIAL. See NUN'S ATTIRE. See BARBE.

GROGRAM—GROGORAM. A ribbed fabric usually of silk, sometimes stiffened with gum.

GUARD. A band of material or lace to serve as trimmin See illus. on page 22.

GUARD—GUARDSMAN'S ATTIRE. "The Queen for her ordinary guard has about one hundred and fifty Englishmen clad in red velvet." (De Maisse.)

See also page 10.

For the attire of the French guard, see text and illus. on page 92.

GUIPURE. See LACE.

GUN (Hand gun).

See HARQUEBUS, CALIVER, MUSKET, SNAPHAUNCE, PETRONEL, CARBINE, PISTOL, DAG, TACKE.

HAIR DRESSING. The illustrations will best explain the manner of dressing the hair. It will be seen that the hair of both men and women was always dressed off the forehead. The women often bleached, dyed and curled their hair, and the wearing of wigs or false parts was not uncommon.

"Correct your frizled locks and in your glasse
Behold the picture of a foolish asse."

(Hutton, *Follie's Anatomie*, 1619.)

"If curling and laying out of their own naturall heyre weare all . . . it were the lesse matter ; but they are not simply contente with their owne haire, but buy other heyre either of Horses, Mares, or any other straunge beastes, dying it of what colour they list themselves." (Stubbes.)

"Her hair is auburn, mine is perfect yellow :
If that be all the difference in his love
I'll get me such a colour'd periwig."

(Shakespeare, *Two Gentlemen*—IV. IV. 196.)

See PERIWIG.

It was the custom for brides in certain localities to wear their hair hanging :

"She was attired all in white, having her hair hanging down at length in faire and seemely tresses." (Stow describing the wedding of the princess Elizabeth to Frederick, Count Palatine.)

The "horn headdress" was a Venetian fashion. For its description see page 17 and illus. on pages 36 and 64.

The "love lock" was a wisp of hair near the left ear, allowed to grow long, sometimes crimped, and of course pure affectation.

"... some by wearing a long locke that hangs dangling by his eare, do think by that lousie commodity to be esteemed by the opinion of foolery." (B. Rich, *Opinion defied*, 1613.)

"Sir, will you have your worship's hair cut after the Italian manner, short and round, and then frounced with the curling-iron, to make it look like a half moon in a mist? Or will you be Frenchified with a love-lock down to your shoulders? wherein you may weave your mistress's favour." (Robert Greene, *A quip for an upstart courtier*, 1592.)

HAIR ORNAMENTS. See illustrations. See pages 16 and 17.

HALBARD — HALBERD — HALBERT. A weapon usually in the form of a battle axe and pike at the end of a long staff, but sometimes in grotesque forms with many points and edges for cutting and thrusting. The blade was often perforated and richly adorned. (*Standard Dictionary*.)

"The Halbardier . . . ought of duty to attend with his halberd when his turne comes about his Ensigne, in marching and set squares, and the Captaines lodging and tent for his guard, and at the entrance of a house etc. and be the foremost person to force the passage." (Edward Davies, *England's Trainings*, 1619.)

". . . Because the Frenchmen make their Halberds with long nickt pikes, and of naughtie stuffe like our common browne bills . . . let the halberds be of good stuffe and stronglie made, after the Millaine fashion, with large heads to cut, and broad strong pikes both to cut and to thrust, then without doubt the halberd is nothing behinde the bill for all manner of service, and armes a souldier fairer than a bill. Both bills and halberds ought to have corslets with light millian murrianes, the forepart ought to be of reasonable proofe, I meane of the proofe of a Caliver discharged 10-12 score . . ." (Sir Roger Williams, *A briefe discourse of warre*, 1590.)

HALBARDIER. One who carries the halbard. See above.

HANDKERCHIEF—HANDKERCHER. Also called MUCKINDER.

"VI handkerchers wrought with black worke, with a border of Venice gold and silver pasmane lace." (New Year's Gift presented to Queen Elizabeth. Nichols' *Progresses of Queen Elizabeth*.)

See illus. on page 38.

HAND-RUFF—RUFFLE—RUFF—CUFF. As the name implies, a ruff at the wrist, usually corresponding with the neck ruff, although often made plain and turned back, when it was usually called a cuff.

HANGERS. An arrangement of straps hanging from the girdle and holding the sword. See CARRIAGES.

HARLEQUINADE (COMMEDIA DELL'ARTE). "In distinction to the written comedies the Commedia dell 'Arte was not and could not be performed except by professional actors. Of a drama only the outline or "Scenario" was traced, the rest being entrusted to the improvisation of the actors—and the rest was everything." (*The Mask*, Vol. III, written by Dr. Michele Scherillo.)

See page 28.

HARQUEBUS—ARCUBUS. A matchlock gun. See illus. on page 98.

HARQUEBUSIER. ". . . Some bring in a custom of too much curiositie in arming Hargabusiers, for besides a peece, flaske, tutch box, rapier and dagger, they load them with a heavie shirt of male, and a Burganet: so that by that time they have marched in the heat of the sommer or deepe of the winter ten or twelve English-

miles, they are more apt to rest then ready to fight . . . Wherefore in mine opinion, it is not necessarie that this extraordinarie arming of shot should be used, but in surprises of Townes, Escalades, and assaults of breaches, to defend the souldiers heads from stones . . . so are these armes nothing so necessarie, but rather a burthen more beautifull then beneficiall, and of greater charge then commoditie, especially a shirt of male, which is very dangerous for shot, if a number of those small peeces should bee driven into a man's body by a bullet." (Edward Davies, *England's trainings*, 1619.)

HAT. "Sometimes they use them sharp on the crowne, perking up like a sphere, or shafte of a steeple, standing a quarter of a yard above the crowne of their heades . . . Othersome be flat and broad on their crowne like the battlements of a house. An other sort have round crownes, sometimes with one kinde of bande, sometimes with an other; now blacke, now white, now russet, now red, now greene, now yellowe, now this, now that, never content with one colour or fashion two dayes to an ende . . . some are of silke, some of velvet, some of taffetie, some of sarcenet, some of woolle, and which is more curious, some of a certaine kind of fine haire, far fetched and deare bought, you may bee sure, and so common a thing it is, that everie Servingman, Countreyman, and other, even all indifferently, do weare of these hattes . . .

"They have also Taffeta hattes of all collours quilted, and imbroydered with golde, silver, and silke of sundrie sortes, with monsters, antiques, beastes, foules, and all maner of pictures and images upon them, wonderfull to behold. Besides this, of late there is a new fashion of wearing their Hattes sprung up amongst them, which they father from the Frenchmen, namely to weare them without bandes; but how unseemelie (I will not say Assy) a fashion that is let the wise judge . . . An other sort (as phantasticall as the rest) are content with no kind of Hatt without a great bunche of feathers of diverse and sundrie colours." (Stubbes, *Anatomy of Abuses*.)

Jolye (The Waiting Gentle-Woman): "Will it please you to weare your haires onely, or els to have your French whood?"

Lady: "Give me my whood, for me thinketh it is somewhat colde, and I have a rewme which is falne on the left side of my head. But tarrye, what weather is it?"

Jolye: "Truly Madame it seemeth that this day will be the fayrest day that hath bene this great while."

Lady: "Set up then my French whood and my Border of Rubies, give me an other head attyre: take the key of my closet, and goe fetch my long boxe where I set my Jewels . . . that I used to weare on my head, what is become of my wyer? Where is the haire-cap? Have you any ribans to make knots? Where be the laces for to bind my haires? . . ." (Erondell's *French Garden*, 1605.)

Late in the period the hat brim was often turned up and fastened to the crown with a jewelled brooch or other ornament.

Hat bands were often of silk or metallic rope:

"I had a gold cable hat band . . ." See page 10.

Scarfs of cypress and with fringed ends were also used as hat bands.

"Where is your hat-band? And you, where is the cipres of yours?" (Erondell's *French Garden*, 1605.)

For "cockle hat," see COCKLE.

See CHAPERON, HOOD, CAP, FELT.

HEADPIECE. A helmet or piece of armour for the head. Also any head covering.

HELMET. A defensive cover for the head. Helmets of this period are the following, which are described under their separate headings: ARMET, BURGONET, MORION, CABASSET. For CLOSE HELMET, see page 94.

HERALD'S COAT. ". . . two napkins tacked together and thrown over the shoulders like a herald's coat without sleeves . . ." (Shakespeare, 1st *Henry IV*—IV. II. 47.) See TABARD.

HOLLAND CLOTH. A linen fabric. Among gifts presented to Queen Elizabeth occur : " Two handkerchers of Holland . . . " "A smock of fyne Holland." " 4 tothclothes of course Hollande." See Moryson's account of Holland, page 15.

HOOD. (a) French Hood. A close fitting bonnet, sometimes having a flat band of material laid from front to back and either trailing down the back or thrown over the head. The front of the hood was usually trimmed with revers, or flaring arches, wired or jewelled, and pressed into a variety of shapes. This is the sort of hood usually associated with Mary Stuart.

　　See Chaperon. See Hat.

　　(b) Ecclesiastical hood or caputium was usually seen upon the scapular and the mozetta. See page 85.

　　(c) Academic hood. See page 83.

　　(d) Casting hood. See page 80.

　　(e) Hood with cape and long tail-like elongation of the peak, may be seen worn on the head or slung over the left shoulder by mourners at the funeral of Sir Philip Sidney. See page 80.

HOOP. See Farthingale.

HORSEMEN. " Most of the horsemen that I met (betwixt Vicenza and Verona) were furnished with muskets, ready charged, and touch-boxes hanging by their sides full of Gunpowder, together with little pouches full of bullets, which is a thing so commonly used in most places of Italie, that a man shall scarce finde a horseman in any place riding without them . . . " (Coryat, *Crudities*, 1611.)

HOSE—HOSYN—HOSEN. This word had at this time three distinct meanings :

　　(a) Stockings and breeches when joined together as one garment. Alluded to as " upper stocks " and " nether stocks."

　　(b) Breeches alone.

　　(c) Stockings alone.

HUKE. " A mantle such as women use in Spain, Germanie, and the low countries, when they goe abroad." (J. Minsheu, *The guide unto tongues*, 1617.) See Moryson under " Netherlands," page 15.

INFULA. The scarf fastened upon the crosier. Also called Vexillum. See illus. on page 86.

INFULÆ. Strings or lappets appended to the back of the mitre.

INKLE—INCLE. Linen tape.

　　" Take an Incle, or Ribband." (Markham, *Caval.*)

JACK. A soldier's jacket, flexible and bullet-proof.

　　" . . . Jackes quilted and covered over with leather, fustian, or canvas, over thicke plates of iron that are sowed in the same." (Harrison's *Description of England*.)

　　The jack, though less costly and without the rivets, served the same purpose as the brigandine.

JACKET—JERKIN. " A comone garmente daylye used such as we call a Jerkin or Jacket withoute sleves." (Thynne, *Animadv.*, 1599.)

　　A garment with or without sleeves worn over the doublet, usually the same cut as the doublet, often made of leather.

　　" A leather Jerkin perfumed with Ambar." (Cervantes, *Don Quixote*, tr. Shelton, 1612.) See illus. on page 26.

JERKIN. See above. See Perfume.

JERSEY — JARZIE — JARNSEY — JARSEY. The knitting of stockings and other worsted articles was an industry of Jersey.

　　" . . . Nether stocks . . . not of cloth . . . for that is thought to base, but of Jarnsey worsted." (Stubbes, *Anatomy of Abuses*.)

JEWELLERY. " Their fingers are decked with gold, silver and precious stones, their wristes with bracelets and armlets of gold, and other precieous Jewels." (Stubbes, *Anatomy of Abuses*.)

　　See Carcanet, Chain, Bracelet, Earring, Brooch Necklace, Billament, Pin, Watch, Ring, Pomander.

Among the gifts received by Queen Elizabeth are lists of jewellery described in full. (See Nichols' *Progresses of Queen Elizabeth*.)

JORNET. A kind of cloak. (Hal.)

JUDGE'S ATTIRE. (1) Usual habit :—

　　Black or violet gown,

　　cape and hood of same colour, ends of hood hanging over behind.

　　　white coif, velvet cap, and cornered caps,

　　　mantle of black or violet.

　　The gown, hood, and mantle faced with taffeta or with white fur of Miniver, according to season.

　　(2) Formal habit :—

　　Scarlet gown and mantle, faced with taffeta or Miniver according to season.

　　　tippet and casting hood worn on right side above the tippet, and the hood is pinned toward left shoulder.

　　　velvet caps, white coyfe and cornered caps.

　　(3) When riding circuit the judges sometimes wore serjeants coats of broadcloth with sleeves, faced with velvet.

　　(The foregoing is a simplified extract of the ordinance of 1635; the complete ruling is to be found in W. Dugdale's *Origines Juridiciales*, 1671.)

KENDAL—KENDAL GREEN. A kind of green woollen cloth made at Kendal in Westmoreland (Onions, *Glossary*.)

　　" Why, how couldst thou know these men in Kendal green, when it was so dark thou couldst not see thy hand ? " (Shakespeare, 1st *Henry IV*—II. 4. 260.)

KENTISH CLOTH. Of Kentish manufacture.

KERCHIEF—KERCHER. A head or neck scarf.

KERSEY — KARSEY — KERSEYE — CARSY — CARSIE. A kind of coarse narrow cloth, woven from long wool and usually ribbed. (*O.E.D.*)

　　" . . . with a linen stock on one leg and a kersey boot-hose on the other." (Shakespeare, *Taming of the Shrew*—III. II. 68.)

KIRTLE—KYRTILL. The kirtle was that visible garment which women wore under the upper gown or the robe or mantle. It might be a complete garment or an upper body, but was more generally a skirt.

　　" But which is more vayn, of whatsoever their petti cots be, yet must they have kyrtles (for so they call them), eyther of silk, velvet, grograin, taffatie, saten, or scarlet, bordered with gards, lace, fringe, and I cannot tell what besydes." (Stubbes, *Anatomy of Abuses*.)

　　In the wardrobe accounts and among the gifts received by Queen Elizabeth there are many allusions to the kirtle (See Nichols' *Progresses*) : " a foreparte and a peir of boddys of a French kyrtill," " trayne of a French kyrtill," " parte of a rounde kyrtill."

　　See illus. on pages 23 and 58.

KNIFE. See illus. on page 35. See Dagger

KNIGHTHOOD ORDERS. William Segar in his full descriptions of the orders in *Honor, military and civill*, 1602, says : " These five orders, Garter of England, that of the Toizon in Burgundie, that of the St. Michael in France, that of the Annunciation in Savoy, and that of the St. Esprit last erected in France, be reputed most honourable and are adorned with great collars, in token they excell all other degrees of Knighthood."

　　(1) For the Order of the Garter, see illus. and text on page 76.

　　(2) For the collar of the Order of St. Esprit, see illus. and text on page 84.

　　(3) Knights of the Toison D'Or, or Golden Fleece, " the collar of this order is of gold wrought of flames and fulfils with the Torzon hanging thereat." (*Ibid.*) (The torzon is in the form of a sheep suspended by a ribbon about its waist. H. K. M.)

　　(4) Knights of St. Michael. " This order is ornified with a great collar whereat the Image of S. Michael hangeth. The words thereupon are these ' Immensi tremor Ocians." (Segar.) See illus. on page 84.

(5) The order of the Annunciation "The collar appertaining to this order is made of gold, and on it these four letters engraven., F.E.R.T., which signifieth Fortitudo eius Rhodum tenuit. At the said collar hangeth a Tablet wherein is the figure of the Annunciation." (*Ibid.*)

LACE. At this period there were two chief classifications of lace, i.e., needlepoint and bobbin. Lace was often called " Passement," which general term included also trimmings. The needle point was called " passemaines d'aiguille," while bobbin laces were called " passemaines au fuseau."

Under NEEDLEPOINT we have the following :

BURATTO. Hand woven canvas in which the threads of the warp are twisted each time the weft thread passes from side to side through the warp. The design is worked with needle point on this surface. It is made on a loom.

CUT LINEN WORK. Groups of counted threads are removed by cutting, in preparation for button hole work and embroidery.

DRAWNWORK. The field for decoration is obtained by withdrawing threads from a piece of linen. This type is sometimes called " Lacis " or " Reticello," meaning geometric.

GUIPURE. A kind of gold and silver thread lace, or passement or braid made with twisted silk, thick cord around which silk is rolled. Mrs. Palliser believed that the English term for guipure might have been " parchment lace," for parchment instead of thread could have been used as a foundation. Cotgrave said, " guipure—a grosse black thread covered or whipped about with silk."

FILET. Square mesh with knots at the corner of each square. In this the design is darned. This was called " net work " or " reseuil," and was made on a frame. Net work or reseuil were not necessarily square mesh, but might be diamond mesh.

PARCHMENT. Toward 1600 lace began to be made over cloth backed parchment on which an outlining thread was couched serving as a supporting framework for the pattern. The design was worked on the surface, not through the parchment.

The second classification is BOBBIN LACE, or pillow lace. At this period it was often called " bone lace," it is believed because the pins were made of fish bones. This lace was made with pins and bobbins over a pillow. See BONE-LACE.

A few other terms under lace, met with at this period are :—

A purle edge, which was a narrow edging of projecting loops, to be sewn upon lace as a finish at the border.

Billement lace applied chiefly to metal or mixed metal and silk lace. Its name died out during this period.

Compas lace—having a circular pattern.

Crowns lace—having crowns worked in its design.

The word LACE had in addition to the above the following meanings :—

A lace—a string or cord.

A lace—ornamental banding or trimming.

To lace—to fasten or to tighten.

To lace—to ornament or to trim with lace.

See BRIDE LACE, see TAWDRY LACE.

For detailed study of the subject of lace see *History of Lace*, by Mrs. Bury Palliser, edited by Jourdain and Dryden, 1910. See also an excellent article in the *Encyclopædia Britannica*, 14th Edition.

LANCE. The war lance was a long wooden shaft with an iron or steel head, held by horsemen in charging at full speed.

See CAVALRY. The tilt yard lance may be seen illustrated on pages 92 and 95.

LANCE REST. A steel bracket affixed to the right side of the breast plate as a support for the lance.

LAPPET. See INFULÆ. See MITRE.

LATCH. A cross-bow. See BOW, CROSS-BOW.

LATCHET. Fastening for shoes.

LAWN. A delicate fabric resembling fine linen or cambric of which ruffs, cuffs, handkerchiefs, aprons or shirts were made.

" In the third yeere of the rayne of Queene Elizabeth, 1562, beganne the knowledge and wearing of Lawne and Cambrick, which was then brought into England." (Stow's *Annales*.) See STARCH.

LEGAL ATTIRE. See JUDGE. See SERJEANT.

Regulations regarding the attire at the Inns of Court during this period are as follows :—

" That they go not in cloaks, hats, boots, and spurs into the city, but when they ride out of town.

No fellow of the house should come into the Hall with any weapon, except his dagger or his knife.

No great ruffs should be worn.

Nor any white colour in doublets or hosen.

Nor any facing of velvet in gowns but by such as were of the bench.

That no hats or curled hair be worn.

Nor any gowns but such as were of a sad colour.

No gentlemen of the society do go into the city or suburbs or to walk in the fields otherwise than in his gown.

No gentlemen of the society do come into the Hall to any meal with their hats, boots or spurs, but with caps."

(W. Dugdale's *Origines Juridiciales*, 1671.)

LINCOLN GREEN. The best green was dyed in Lincoln.

" All in a woodman's jacket he was clad of Lincolne green." (Spenser's *Faerie Queene*, 1589-90.)

LINEN. Fabric woven from flax. See Moryson's account of the Netherlands on page 15.

LINSEY-WOOLSEY. A course woollen stuff first manufactured at Linsey in Suffolk. (Planché.)

LINSTOCK. A pike with branches on each side, sometimes formed in the shape of a bird's head, to hold a lighted match for the cannoneer who used it, and was thus capable of defending himself with the same impliment. (Fairholt.)

" . . . and the nimble gunner
With linstock now the devilish cannon touches."
(Shakespeare, *Henry V*—III, Prologue, 32.)

LIVERY. Uniform of servants and retainers, officials or members of a company.

" . . . They (the English) keep many retainers, for the most part portly and good-looking men who go without cloaks, but have only Jerkins of their lord's colour, and bearing his arms rolled up and buckled behind : they likewise have the same arms upon their sleeves, so that they may be distinguished." (Rathgeb, written 1602, Rye.)

(To a tavern serving man) : ". . . look you, Francis, your white canvas doublet will sully." (Shakespeare, 1st *Henry IV*—II. IV. 84.)

(Regarding the servants) " Let their heads be sleekly combed, their blue coats brushed, and their garters of an indifferent knit (quiet colour)." (Shakespeare, *Taming of the Shrew*—IV. I. 93.)

" The servants of Gentlemen were wont to weare blew coates, with their Masters badge of silver on the left sleeve : but now they most commonly weare clokes garded with lace, all the servants of one family wearing the same livery for colour and ornament ; and for the rest, are apparrelled with no lesse pride and inconstancie of fashion then other degrees." (Moryson on England, 1617.)

" . . . executioner dressed in black velvet . . . " (in a letter to Henri III from the French Ambassador concerning execution of Mary Stuart, from Stricklands' *Letters of Mary Queen of Scots*).

See SWORD. See MANDILION.

LOCK. See HAIR.

LOCKRAM. A linen fabric.

"I can wet one of my newe Lockeram napkins with weeping." (Greene, *Never too late*, 1590.)

"His ruffe was of fine lockeram." (Greene, *Greene's vision*, 1592.)

LONG-BOW. See Bow.

LOOKING GLASS. ". . . they must have their looking glasses carryed with them wheresoever they go. And good reason, for els how could they see the devil in them?" (Stubbes, *Anatomy of Abuses*.)

". . . a faire large looking glasse set in frame, corded with crimson velvett, bound with a passamayn lace of Venis gold." (New Year's gift to Queen Elizabeth. Nichol's *Progresses of Queen Elizabeth*.)

See Mirror. See illus. and text on page 59.

LOVE-LOCK. A masculine mode of hair dress. See Hair.

MACE. A short ornamental baton borne before dignitaries, held by certain officials.

MAIL. The name for all metal armour not composed of large plates.

"to hang quite out of fashion, like a rusty mail." (Shakespeare, *Troilus and Cressida*—III. III. 152.)

". . . A shirt of male, which is very dangerous for shot, if a number of those small peeces should bee driven into a man's body by a bullet." (Davies' *England's Trainings*, 1619.)

According to the above it will be seen that mail was no longer deemed practicable.

See also illus. on page 91 showing that mail was still in use.

MALE. A hole for the passage of a lace.

"Orbiculus—A male or rundle through which the latchet of the shoe passeth." (Thomas, *Dictionary*, 1588.)

MANDILION — MANDEVILE. A short loose outer coat whose under arm seam was unsewn from hem to arm pit and sometimes also from arm pit to wrist.

"Mandilion—a loose cassocke, such as souldiers use to weare." (Minsheu, *Guide unto tongues*, 1617.)

"A garment made like a church tunic with unsewn sleeves but laid over the arm, which could be fastened on the wrists and closed with button or hook." (Claude Hatton, as quoted by Quicherat.)

When Queen Elizabeth continued her progresses to Norwich in 1578, as had been arranged by statute, ". . . threescore of the most comelie yong men of the citie, as bachelers apparelled all in black sattyn doublets, blacke hose, blacke taffeta hattes and yeallowe bandes, and their universall liverie was a mandylion of purple taffeta, layde aboute with silver lace . . ." Nichols' *Progresses of Queen Elizabeth*.)

MANIPLE. A band of material from two to four feet long and two to three inches wide, worn suspended from the left arm near the wrist by officiating clergy, deacon and sub-deacon. See illus. on page 86.

MANTLE. See Robe.

MASK. "When they use to ride abrod, they have masks and visors made of velvet, wherwith they cover all their faces, having holes made in them against their eyes, whereout they look. So that if a man that knew not their guise before, should chaunce to meet one of them, hee would think hee met a monster or a devil; for face hee can see none, but two brode holes against their eyes with glasses in them." (Stubbes, *Anatomy of Abuses*.)

"The great ladies do go well masked, and indeed it be the only show of their modesty to conceal their countenance." (Harington's *Nugæ Antiquæ*.)

"Maskes for faces and for noses." (Shakespeare, *Winter's Tale*—IV. III. 223.)

"But since she did neglect her looking-glass
And threw her sun-expelling mask away,
The air hath starv'd the roses in her cheeks
And pinch'd the lily-tincture of her face."

(Shakespeare, *Two Gentlemen of Verona*—IV. IV. 159.)

See allusion under Chaperon.

MATCHLOCK. A hand gun such as the harquebus, the musket or the carbine, which had affixed to it a cock to hold the match, which was brought down to the priming by a trigger.

MATERIAL. See Fabric.

MINEVOR CAP. See Cap.

MINISTER. ". . . a square cap, a scholar's gown priestlike, a tippet, and in the church a linen surplice." (1564, a proclamation for Ministers as quoted by Strype in his *Life of Grindal*.)

See Sword. See Tippet.

MINIVER. "Miniver is nothing but the bellies of squirrels, as some men say, others say it is a little vermine like unto a Wesel, milke white and commeth from Muscovee." (Minsheu's *Guide unto tongues*, 1617.)

See Robe.

MIRROR. Women wore mirrors at their girdles, in brooches and in their fans.

"One fanne of feathers of divers colours, the handle of golde . . . and a looking glasse on th'one side." (Queen Elizabeth's wardrobe, 1600. Nichols' *Progresses*.)

According to the following, men wore mirrors in their hats:

"Call for your casting-bottle and place your mirror in your hat as I told you." (Ben Jonson's *Cynthia's revels*, 1601.)

MITRE. A peaked ecclesiastical headdress worn on solemn occasions by Pope, Bishops, Cardinals, Abbots of some monasteries, and from special privilege by the canons of certain churches.

(a) Mitre Simplex—white linen or silk, little or no enrichment.

(b) Mitre Aurefrigiata—richly embroidered, but without jewels.

(c) Mitre Pretiosa — richly embroidered with precious metals and jewels.

The two streamers that hang side by side down the back of the mitre are called lappets or infulæ. (Macalister, *Ecclesiastical Vestments*, 1896.)

In the Anglican church after the Reformation the mitre was seldom worn except upon that rare occasion, a coronation. In Nichols' *Progresses*, the coronation of Queen Elizabeth is described as follows: " In the hall they met the bishop that was to perform the ceremony, and all the chappel, with three crosses born before them, in their copes, the bishop mitred."

For illustrations of the Mitre, see pages 85, 86 and 87.

MOCKADO—MOCHADO—MOKKADO. A kind of woollen stuff, made in imitation of velvet, and sometimes called mock-velvet. (Hal.)

MOCKETER—MOCKET—MUCKINDER. A bib, a handkerchief.

"Where is his bibbe? Let him have his gathered Aprone with stringes, and hang a Muckinder to it." (Erondell's *French Garden*, 1605.)

See Bavarette.

MOILE. See Moyles.

MONASTIC ORDERS. Below is a selected list of religious orders, together with their distinguishing attire :—

Augustine, St. Black tunic, girded, black cape and hood. White might be worn indoors.

Benedict, St. Black woollen tunic to which a caputium is sewn, scapular, cuculla from shoulder to feet with very wide sleeves.

Capuchins. Rough black woollen tunic girded with coarse rope; hood and cape, sandals.

Carmelites. Tunic, girdle, scapular, caputium, brown; cappa or mantle, white. Hat on head black except in Mantua, where it is white. At Monte Sacro the cappa is shorter and no cap on head at any time.

Carthusians. Black woollen pallium, over which a white gown was passed over the head, and a scapular with side loops.

CISTERCIANS (Trappists). White cuculla with ample sleeves, girded, caputium.

DOMINIC, ST. (Black Friars). Tunic, scapular, and broad round caputium of white wool. Black cappa, shorter than the tunic, added for out of doors.

FRANCISCANS (de observantia). Woollen tunic girded with cord ; cape, hood, colour formed by mixture of two parts of black wool to one of white ; wooden or leather sandals. (Those of St. Peter of Alcantara wore rough and patched tunic girded with cord, a cape and a hood, with feet entirely unprotected. Macalister's *Ecclesiastical Vestments*, 1896.)

For further information upon this subject, the following comprehensive and carefully illustrated work is unsurpassed : Philippo Bonanni, *Catalogo degli ordini religiosi*, in five volumes, containing hundreds of full page engravings of monks and nuns.

MONIAL. An enamelled or jewelled disc set into the ecclesiastical glove. See illus. on page 85.

MONMOUTH CAP. See CAP.

MORION. A light helmet for infantry. It had neither visor nor beaver.

For COMB MORION see page 91.

For CABASSET (or SPANISH MORION), see illus. on page 97.

MORRIS DANCER'S ATTIRE.

"Clod : They should be morris-dancers by their gingle, but they have no napkins.

Cock : No, nor a hobby-horse.

Clod : But there is no Maid Marian nor Friar amongst them . . .

Cock : Nor a fool that I see.

Clod : Unless they be all fools."

(Ben Jonson's *Every Man out of his Humour*, 1600.)

MORRIS PIKE. A form of pike said to be of Moorish origin.

MORSE. A brooch which fastened the cope. See illus. on page 85.

MOTLEY. Cloak bags were made of motley cloth. Motley meant also parti-coloured or diversified in colour, fool's dress :

"Oh, that I were a fool ! I am ambitious for a motley coat." (Shakespeare, *As you Like It*—II. VII. 43.)

MOURNING ATTIRE. Under " Mourning Robes " in Queen Elizabeth's wardrobe accounts all articles mentioned are of " purple vellat." (See Nichols' *Progresses of Queen Elizabeth*.)

" . . . The Queen in black because she is in mourning for the Prince of Orange and the Duke of Alençon." (Letters of Von Wedel, 1585, edited by Klarwill.)

See BARBE. See illus. on page 78.

Vecellio mentions mourning attire in a number of instances. Sometimes a black veil is worn over the head and face. " . . . Widows cover their chest with a tight veil, wear a black shawl over their heads, and to the forehead . . . If they wish to remain widows they wear a train (strascino). In the house they wear a coiffe (scuffietta) which covers their hair . . . They are always dressed in black. If they wish to remarry, they may, without incurring blame, wear a few ornaments, and uncover slightly their hair. This makes known their intentions to those who see them." (Vecellio's *Abiti*, 1590, Vol. I, Plate 109.)

" After them followed more than five hundred poore men in long mourning gownes from the top to the toe, with hoods over their heads." (Funeral observations of the Kings of France, in Andrew Favine's *Theatre of Honour*, 1620.)

MOUSTACHE — MOUCHADO — MOWCHATOWE

" Your moustachios sharp at the ends like shoemakers awls or hanging down to your mouth like goats flakes." (Lyly's *Midas*, 1592.)

See page 26.

MOYLES—MOILES—MULES. " Mules, also moyles, pantofles, high slippers." (Cotgrave.)

" Thou wear'st (to weare thy wyt and thrift together) Moyles of velvet to save thy shooes of lether ; Ofte have we seene moyle men ryde uppon asses, But to see assys go on moyles, that passys ! "

(J. Heywood, 1587, as quoted by Fairholt.)

MOZETTA. Cardinal's cape. See illus. on page 88.

MUCKINDER. Handkerchief. See MOCKETER.

MUFF. Also called SNUFFKIN, SNOUSKIN, SKIMSKYN. These were worn by women, were usually small, and were sometimes appended by a long cord from the waist. Numerous allusions are made to " Skimskyns " under New Year's gifts to Queen Elizabeth in Nichols' *Progresses of Queen Elizabeth* :

" Skimskin of watched satten, ymbrodered with knotts and Venis gold and lyned with carnation plushe," and another of cloth of silver " ymbrodered all over with beasts and flowers and a woman in the middst."

" . . . for I must buye a silke waste-coat which I have lost in play . . . against a velvet Muffe." (Erondell's *French Garden*, 1605.)

MUFFLER. " A kerchief or like thing that men and women used to wear about their necke and cheekes . . . " (Baret, 1580.)

MULES. See MOYLES.

MUSKET. A large heavy matchlock gun. See HORSEMEN. The musket was primarily an infantry firearm. See illus. and text on page 99.

MUSKET REST. A staff with forked head upon which to rest the musket when firing. The furrelled end was thrust into the ground. See page 99.

NAPKIN. Term sometimes used for pocket handkerchief. " Oft did she heave her napkin to her eyne." (Shakespeare, *A Lover's Complaint*.)

NECKERCHIEF. As the name implies, a kerchief for the neck.

NECKLACE. Various types of necklaces may be studied in the portraits. See CARCANET.

NETHER-STOCKS. Another term for stockings. See STOCKINGS. See HOSE.

NIGHT CAP. Also called NIGHT COYFE. " A knit night-cap made of the coarsest twine, With two long labels buttoned to his chin."

(Hall's *Satires*, 1597.)

" White quilted linnen night cap." (Cervantes, *Don Quixote*, tr. Shelton, 1612.)

Presented to Queen Elizabeth by Fowlke Grevell, " A smock of camerick wrought abowte the coller and sleves of Spanyshe worke of roses and tres, and a night coyf with a forehed clothe of the same worke." (Nichols' *Progresses*, under New Year's Gifts, 1577-8.)

NIGHT GOWN. A dressing gown or what to-day might be called tea gown. What was worn during the night was probably a smock, often alluded to as " night attire."

The lady is arising and addresses her maid, " . . . why doe you not give me my nightgowne ? For I take colde . . . Undoe my night attire." (Erondell's *French Garden*, 1605.)

De Maisse, in reference to Elizabeth's appearance upon his first audience with her, says : " She excused herself because I found her attired in her nightgown." He describes her attire minutely, fabric, colour, sleeves, collar ornamentation, etc. (*Journal of De Maisse*, 1597.)

" . . . I have seen her rise from her bed, throw her night-gown upon her . . . " (Shakespeare, *Macbeth*—V. I. 5.)

NIGHT RAIL. " Un collet à peignoir—a large raile which women put about their neckes when they combe themselves." (Cotgrave.)

" A nightrail of camberick, wroughte all over with black silke." (Gift to Queen Elizabeth, as quoted in Nichols' *Progresses of Queen Elizabeth*.)

NUNS ATTIRE. The general habit was a gown or tunic (vestes), girt at waist, and a scapular. They usually wore a white gremial, *i.e.*, breast cloth (see BARBE) fastened over the head and round the throat and breast. Over this two loose vela, or cloths, are placed over the head, the inner white, the outer black. Feet are rarely unprotected. (Macalister's *Ecclesiastical Vestments*.)

OREILLETTES. Movable steel ear coverings affixed to the open tilting or coursing helmet. They might be lifted by means of a hinge.

ORPHREYS. Bands of embroidery, usually gold, to be seen on such vestments as cope and chasuble. See illus. on page 87. The Y-shaped orphrey should not be confounded with the PALL.

OVERSHOE. See CHOPINES, MOYLES, PANTOFLES, PATTENS.

PAINT. See COSMETICS.

PALL or PALLIUM. (*a*) White woollen woven band encircling the shoulders, and having two tails before and two behind. This was worn by the Pope, and by him bestowed upon all Archbishops. It was worn at high mass by the Archbishop and by the Pope at all times when saying Mass. See illus. page 85.

(*b*) A cloak with a hood, worn by monks.
See MONASTIC ORDERS.

PAMPILION. A kind of fur. See FUR.
Also a coat of different colours, formerly worn by servants. (Hollyband's *Dictionary*, 1593.)

PANES. Parallel cuts made in garments, particularly in men's breeches through which the lining might be seen or pulled through. The panes gave the effect of being parallel bands or guards often elaborately decorated.

King James's embroiderer received 320 pearls " for the panes of his Ma'ts hose." (Nichols' *Progresses of King James*, year 1606.)
See illus. on pages 46 and 80. See page 11.

PANTALOON. A character in the old Italian popular comedy. See illus. on page 28.
See HARLEQUINADE.
" . . . the lean and slipper'd pantaloon,
With spectacles on nose and pouch on side."
(Shakespeare, *As You Like It*—II. VII. 158.)

PANTOFLE—PANTOBLE—PANTACLE. A slipper for indoors, also used out of doors as a protection to the delicate shoes.
" Pull off my shooes, give me my pantofles, and my night gowne." (Erondell's *French Garden*, 1605.)
" . . . fine pantofles which beare them up two inches or more from the ground." (Stubbes, *Anatomy*.)
See illus. on pages 28, 30 and 38.

PARCHMENT LACE. See LACE.

PARLIAMENT ROBES. See page 89. See ROBE.

PARTISAN. Pole arms, used as a military weapon, or as a leading staff by civic or other guards.
" A partisan—a javeline to skirmish with." (Elyot, 1538.)
" The lieutenant should carry a fair gilt partisan richly trimmed, not being above twelve inches of blade, sharp and well steeled." (Markham, *Five Decades*.)
In Shakespeare's *Hamlet*, Marcellus, an officer, in reference to the ghost, says, " Shall I strike it with my partisan ? " (I. I. 140.)

PARTLET. " A neckerchief or partlet." (Baret, 1580.)
In Hollyband's *Treasury of the French Tongue* we find : " Un collet ou gorgias de quoy les femmes couvrent leur poictrines, a partlet."
The partlet is frequently mentioned among the gifts to Queen Elizabeth. (Nichols' *Progresses*.)
" Partlett and a peire of sleeves of cypres " ; " partlett of gold and silver knytt " ; " A pertelet of fyne camerike " ; " A partelet and ruffe of lawne."

PASSEMENT or PASSEMAINE. See LACE.

PASTORAL STAFF. See CROSIER.

PATTEN. A shoe or overshoe whose purpose it was to raise the foot off the ground for one reason or another, by means of metal, cork, or wood.
Moryson calls " skating," " sliding on pattens." (*Itinerary*, 1617.)
Brantôme in describing a woman of fashion says " your great patins a foot high." (*Mémoires*.)
" . . . irons to be tied under shoes to keep them out of dirt." (Randal Holme, 1688.)
" Zoccoli—wooden pattens, clogs, chopines, galashoes." (Florio.)
Clog, moyle, pantofle or chopine could all be classed as " pattens." See those words.

PAULDRONS. Shoulder pieces in plate armour. See page 94.

PEARLS. The profuse use of pearls by those who could afford them may be studied throughout the illustrations. See PANES.

PEER'S ROBES. See illus. on page 89. See ROBE.

PENISTONES. A kind of coarse woollen cloth.

PERFUME. " Is not this a certen sweete Pride to have cyvet, muske, sweete powders, fragrant Pomanders, odorous perfumes, and such like, whereof the smel may be felt . . . not only all over the house, or place where they be present . . . " (Stubbes, *Anatomy*.)
" . . . neyther could they make any costly wash or perfume until about the fourteenth or fifteenth yeare of the queene the right honorable Edward de Vere, Earl of Oxford, came from Italy, and brought with him gloves : sweete bagges, a perfumed leather Jerkin and other pleasant thinges." (Stow's *Annales*.)

PERIWIG—PEREWYKE (PERUKE.) False hair, false pieces or entire wigs worn by women and occasionally by men.
" She [Mary Seaton] did set sotche a curled Heare upon the Queen [Mary Stuart] that was said to be a Perewyke, that shoed very delycately." (Sir Francis Knollys, 1568. Letter to Cecil as quoted in *O.E.D.*)
" Th'unruly winde blowes off his periwinke." Bishop Hall, 1598, *Satires*, III as quoted in *O.E.D.*)
De Maisse (1597) in describing Elizabeth mentions her " great reddish coloured periwig." Hentzner (1598) says " She wore false hair, and that red." See page 9.
See HAIR DRESSING.

PERPETUANA. A durable fabric of wool.
A kind of glossy cloth generally called everlasting. (Hal.)

PETRONEL. A firearm, smaller than the harquebus and larger than the pistol. " A Petranell, or horseman's peece." (Barret, *Theorike of warres*, 1598.)

PETTICOAT. " Then have they Petticots of the best cloth that can be bought, and of the fairest dye that can be made." (Stubbes, *Anatomy of Abuses*.)
" Bring me my petty-coate bodyes : I meane my damask quilt bodies with whale bones . . . . Give me my peticoate of wroughte Crimson velvet with silver fringe." (Erondell's *French Garden*, 1605.)
The petticoats at times reveal themselves at the hem of the gown, or the gown is deliberately raised to show them.
When the gown is open up the front, the petticoat or kirtle is again revealed. See pages 67 and 23.
" Item one peticoate of crimson golde tinsell striped with a garde of blewe vellat embrodered with Venice silver." (Wardrobe accounts of Queen Elizabeth, Folger MS., 273, 1.)

PICKADIL—PICCARDILL. According to contemporary testimony, the pickadil was that kind of collar support which was made in the form of a series of square or oblong tabs. This term applied not necessarily to the collar support, but might be the tabbed edge to the skirts of a doublet or jerkin, or the finish to the edge of any garment, provided it were tabbed. See Cotgrave who says : " Piccadilles, the severall divisions or peeces fastened together about the brimme of a collar of a doublet, etc." Minsheu has : " tacinia, quæ vestis lacerats, ora et extremitas vestimentı." (*Guide unto tongues*, 1617.) See illus. on page 74.

PIKE. Pole arm used by infantry. The staff was from twelve to eighteen feet long topped with a steel piercing weapon.

"For the plaine field, neither . . . Halberd, nor Partizan comparable to the Pike." (Barret, *Theorike of warres*, 1598.)

" . . . he ought to have his pike at the point and midest trimmed with handsome tassels, and a handle, not so much for ornament as to defend the Souldiers body from water, which in rain doth runne downe alongst the wood." (Davies' *England's Trainings*, 1619.)

See illus. on pages 97 and 100 and accompanying text.

PILCH. An outer garment generally worn in cold weather and made of skins of fur. (Hal.)

Also applied to buff or leather jerkins. (*Ibid.*)

PILEUS. Academic hat. A plain skull cap or a round brimless cap with a point in the centre.

See CAP.

PIN. "About this time (1570) Englishmen began to make all sorts of Pinnes . . ." (Stow's *Annales*, E. Howes, 1615.)

"Is there no small pinnes for my Cuffes ? Look in the pinne-cushen. Pinne that with a blacke pinne . . ." (Erondell's *French Garden*, 1605.)

" . . . give me that Rebato as it is, I will pin it anone . . ." (*Ibid.*)

PINKING. Ornamentation made by puncturing material in a design.

" . . . A velvet or a taffatie Hatte and that muste bee pincked and cunningly carved of the beste fashion." (Stubbes, *Anatomy of Abuses*.)

" . . . her pinked porringer fell off her head." (Shakespeare, *Henry VIII*—V. IV. 51.)

See illus. on pages 26 and 46.

PINSONS—PINSNETS—PISNETS. "A pumpe or pinsen to weare in pantofles." (Minsheu, *Xervilla*, 1599, as quoted in *Oxford Dictionary*.) Probably a very delicate shoe requiring the protection of a pantofle.

PIPE. " In these daies, the taking-in of the smoke of the Indian herbe called ' Tabaco,' by an instrument formed like a litle ladell, wherby it passeth from the mouth into the hed & stomach, is gretlie taken-up & used in England, against Rewmes & some other diseases ingendred in the longes & inward partes, & not without effect." (Harrison's *Chronologie*, 1573.)

Hedge : " Mistress, will you drink a pipe of tobacco ? "

Margery : " Oh, fie upon it, Roger, perdy ! These filthy tobacco pipes are the most idle slavering baubles that ever I felt. Out upon it, God bless us, men look not like men that use them."

See TOBACCO BOX.

PISTOL. The pistol came into use in the sixteenth century.

For other short, light fire arms, see DAG, PETRONEL, CARBINE, TACKE.

PLACKET. A slit in the seam of a skirt or petticoat, or a petticoat itself. Also the wearer of a petticoat, or a woman.

PLASTERON. "Armed men, most carry the pike, having plasterons of the proofe, I mean the forepart of the armour." (Roger Williams, *Brief discourse*, 1590.)

PLATE. Plate armour, or armour not formed of scales or rings.

PLOMMETTES. A fabric. Fairholt says it is probably identical with CARRELLS.

PLUME. These were used in fans, on hats for men and women, and in helmets. See the many examples of plumes among the illustrations.

See FEATHERS.

PLUSH. Many of the muffs presented to Queen Elizabeth were " lyned with white plushe." (See Nichols' *Progresses of Queen Elizabeth*.)

POCKET. " I'll be sworn my pocket was picked." (Shakespeare, 1st *Henry IV*—III. III. 70.)

POINTS. Lacings with metal ends, used instead of buttons or hooks for fastening together such garments as doublet and hose.

" Their points being broken,
Down fell their hose."

(Shakespeare, 1st *Henry IV*—II. IV. 242.)

Points sometimes served no particular purpose other than decorative. See illus. on pages 50 and 79.

POKE. Pocket.

POKING STICK—PUTTING STICK—PUTTER. A rod used for adjusting the pleats of a ruff.

" About the sixteenth yeere of the Queen (1573-4) began the making of steele poking stickes, and untill that time all Lawndresses used setting stickes, made of wood or bone." (E. Howe, 1615, Stow's *Annales*.)

Stubbes (*Anatomy of Abuses*) says, " When they come to starching and setting of their ruffes then must this instrument be heated in the fire, the better to stiffen the ruff." He calls it a " putter " or " putting stick " and says it is made of " yron and steele, and some of brasse kept bright as silver, yea and some of silver it selfe ; and it is well if in processe of time they grow not to be gold."

Bill : " Where's my ruffe and poker you block-head ? Ro.: Your ruffe, your poker, are engendring together upon the cup-bord of the Court, or the Court Cupbord . . . "

(Dekker, *The Honest whore*, 1604.)

See also SETTING STICK.

POLE ARMS. See BILL, GLAIVE, HALBARD, PARTISAN, PIKE.

POMANDER. A metal case usually round, in which was contained a mixture of aromatic substance or perfume. See page 23.

Pomander might also apply to the composition itself, usually in the shape of a ball and carried in the pocket or elsewhere as a preservative against infection. Sometimes it was made in segments, each containing a different perfume.

PONIARD. See DAGGER.

PONTIFICALS. See RING.

POPE. Bishop of Rome. When celebrating pontifically his vestments are : buskins, sandals, amice, alb, girdle, fanon or orale, stole, tunic, dalmatic, gloves, chasuble, pallium, mitre, ring. The maniple is assumed after the confiteor. He does not use the crosier. In ordinary dress he retains rochet and stole. (Pugin.)

POUNCET BOX. A perfume box.

" And 'twixt his finger and his thumb he held
A pouncet box, which ever and anon
He gave his nose and took 't away again."

(Shakespeare, 1st *Henry IV*—I. III. 38.)

POURPOINT. See DOUBLET.

POWDER. See COSMETICS.

POWDER FLASK. Receptacle for gunpowder.

See HARQUEBUSIER. See TOUCH-BOX.

PRIEST'S VESTMENTS. At Mass : Cassock, amice, alb, girdle, maniple, stole and chasuble.

At other sacraments : Surplice and stole. Colour of stole varies. See VESTMENTS.

At vespers and benediction, processions and funerals : Cope over the alb or surplice.

At blessing of the Holy Oils and Procession of Corpus Christi : the assisting priests use chasubles. The stole is used also for preaching and follows colour of the day.

Priests should never quit the ecclesiastical habit, but wear the cassock and the tonsure wherever they appear in public.

The priest is the third of the holy orders whose principal office in church is to offer the Holy Sacrifice, and to administer the Sacraments of Baptism, Penance, Eucharist, Extreme Unction and Matrimony. (Pugin's *Ecclesiastical Ornament*, 1868.)

See TIPPET.

PRIMER. See Touch-Box.

PRIVY COAT. A coat of defence, such as a coat of mail, worn underneath an outer coat. See Corset.

PRODD. A light cross-bow used principally for shooting deer. See Bow.

PROOF ARMOUR. Armour which was bullet proof.

PROVINCIAL ROSE. A rosette for shoes. suggestive in form to the damask rose. See Rose.

See illus. on page 68.

PUKE. A kind of woollen fabric. "Jerkins of fine puke." (Cervantes, *Don Quixote*, tr. Shelton, 1612.)

There was also a colour called "puke." Florio says "a deep dark purple or puke colour," and Baret describes it as "colour betweene russet and blacke."

PULLINGS OUT. Sometimes called "drawings out." An inner lining visible between slashes or cuts, or between panes of a garment. It served a purely decorative purpose.

"A payer of paned hose of bugell panes drawne out with cloth of silver . . ." (Henslowe's *Diary*, 1595.)

See page 11.

"By the Lady Wodhowse LXXIIII flowers made for pullings owte for a peire of slevis wrought with Venice gold and silver." (New Year's Giftes to Queen Elizabeth, Folger MS. 781. 1.)

PUMPS. "Escarpins—Pumpes ; light, or single-soled shooes." (Cotgrave, 1611.)

"Their shoes are not fastened on with lachettes, but lyke a poumpe close aboute the foote." (W. Watreman, *Fardle Facions*, 1555. *O.E.D.*)

PURL. (1) A pleat or flute of a ruff.

"My lord, one of the purls of your band is, without all discipline, fallen out of his rank." (Massinger and Field, *The Fatal Dowry*.)

(2) "Canetille-gold or silver Purle, also a small purle of needle-worke, or a small edging (bone) lace." (Cotgrave.)

PURSE. "Where is my pursse to weare upon my gowne?" (Erondell's *French Garden*, 1605.)

PUTTING STICK. See Poking Stick.

QUERPO. See Cuerpo.

QUILLON. Cross bar of a sword, rapier or dagger.

QUOIF. Close-fitting cap. See Coif.

RAPIER. A light long and narrow sword used rather for thrusting than for cutting. For fighting, the sword or rapier was held in the right hand and the dagger in the left to help ward the blow. This method superseded the sword and buckler fighting. See illustrations.

See Sword.

Hamlet : "What's his weapon?"
Osr.: "Rapier and dagger."
(Shakespeare, *Hamlet*—V. II. 152.)

RASH. Smooth fabric made of silk (silk rash), or worsted (cloth rash). See allusion under Tuft-Taffeta.

RAZE—RACE—RASE. Cuts or slashes in garments as decoration. See illus. on pages 26 and 79.

REBATO—RABATO. "Rabat—a Rebatoe for a woman's ruffe, also a falling band." (Cotgrave, 1611.)

". . . Give me my Rebato of cutworke edged, is not the wyer after the same sorte as the other?" (Erondell's *French Garden*, 1605.)

"In Prussia I observed them to weare long ruffes, with rebatoes of wire to beare them up, such as our women use." (Moryson's *Itinerary*, 1605-17.)

See illus. on page 49.

See Supportasse, Pickadil.

RIBBON. ". . . some silke ribens . . . for to make Roses and knots." (Erondell's *French Garden*, 1605.)

Ribbon was used in the hair, upon the shoes in "roses" or rosettes, as ornamentation to sleeve and gown. It was also worn about the neck to which was then appended a trinket of some sort. The emblem of the order of knighthood was at times appended to a ribbon and worn about the neck. See illus. on page 56.

RING.

"Nor can good Myson weare on his left hand
A signet ring of bristol-diamond ;
But he must cut his glove to show his pride,
That his trim jewel might be better spied."
(Hall's *Satires*, 1597.)

See illus. for numerous examples of rings.

Episcopal Ring (Annulus). A gold circle set with a precious stone, worn by bishop on middle finger of right hand between first and second joint and usually held in place by a guard. It was large enough to permit its passing over the gloved hand. Other rings appearing on the fingers are called pontificals.

"Item, a pontificale of golde with a great saphyer in it of playne worke." (Hierurgia Anglicana.)

ROBE. This term is usually applied to formal attire, such as the outer garment worn on state occasions by sovereigns, peers, officials, etc. In the wardrobe accounts of Queen Elizabeth we find under "Robes" the sub-headings: "Coronation," "Mourning," "Parliament," "For the Order of the Garter." All of the foregoing consist of a mantle, and usually the accompanying kirtle. The mantle is the "loose gown" and the ensemble is called the "robe."

Coronation Robes. These differed from the parliament robes by being of velvet and having capes or tippets of ermine in lieu of bars of miniver. (Augustin Vincent, as quoted by Planché.)

"First a baron of the Parliament is invested in a kirtall of Scarlet girt to his middle, thereupon he putteth his hood . . . and over all his mantle ; and the mantle being on, the end of the hood is pulled out behind the neck and hangeth over the mantell as in the viscount's." (*Ibid.*)

See illus. and text on page 89.

For further contemporary information, consult Selden's *Titles of Honour*, 1614.

Bishop's Robes. "Bishops . . . riding in their robes of scarlet lined, and hoods down their backs of miniver." (Occasion of the Queen's second Parliament, Nichols' *Progresses of Queen Elizabeth*.)

See Knighthood. See Judges.

ROCHET. A kind of modified alb of white linen. The Bishops of the Anglican church wore the chimere over the rochet. See illus. on page 90.

According to Cotgrave the rochet was "a frocke, loose gaberdine or gowne of canvas, or course linnen, worn by a labourer over the rest of his clothes ; also a Prelate's Rochet."

RONDACHE. A shield with aperture for sight, and another for thrusting point of sword.

ROSE. An ornament or rosette, made in the shape of a rose. It was usually made of ribbon and worn upon the shoes. See Shoes.

The rose was worn on hats, in the hair, and as decoration on other garments as well.

A real rose or a rosette was occasionally worn over the ear. See illus. on page 70.

RUFF. "They have great and monsterous ruffes, made either of Cambrick, holland, lawn, or els of some other the finest cloth that can be got for money, whereof some be a quarter of a yard deep, yea, some more, very few lesse ; So that they stand a full quarter of a yarde (and more) from their necks, hanging over their shoulder poynts, insted of a vaile. But if it happen that a shoure of raine catch them before they can get harbour, then their great ruffes strike sayle, and down they fall, as dishcloutes fluttering in the winde, like Windmill sayles." (Stubbes' *Anatomy of Abuses*.)

"(Ruffes) are either clogged with golde, silver, or silk lace of stately price wrought all over with needle woork, speckled and sparkled heer and there with the sonne, the moone, the stares and many other antiquities straunge to beholde. Some are wrought with open woork down to the midst of the ruffe and further, some with lace so cloyd and other gewgawes so pestred, as the ruffe is the least parte of itself. Sometimes they are pinned up to their eares, sometimes they are suffered to hang over their shoulders . . . " (*Ibid.*)

" (They use) a certaine kind of liquide matter which they call Starch, wherein the Devill hath willed them to wash . . . his ruffes wel, which, when they be dry, wil then stand stiffe and inflexible about their necks." He further adds that the starch was " of all colours and hewes, as White, Redde, Blewe, Purple, and the like." (*Ibid.*)

According to contemporary paintings, the coloured ruffs were extremely rare, although yellow seems to have had a certain vogue.

" First to my Laundresse for a yellow band." (S. Rowlands' *A pair of spy-knaves*, 1619.)

" All the women's ruffs are of deepe watchet [blue]." (Sir Richard Wynne at Madrid. Nichols' *Progresses of James I.*)

Punt. (to his servant) : " Sirrah, keep close, yet not so close : thy breath will thaw my ruff." (*Everyman out of his Humour*, B. Jonson, 1600.)

" His Ruffe was of fine lockeram, stitcht very faire with Coventrie blew." (Robert Greene, *Greene's Vision*. 1592.)

By studying the illustrations one may best learn what is meant by a " ruff à la confusion," " cart wheel " and the various forms of this interesting fashion.

It will be noted that though the ruff may be large or small, open or closed, it is rarely seen hanging loose about the throat. In connection with ruff, see FALL, BAND, PICKADIL, SUPPORTASSE, STARCH.

RUFF CUFF—HAND RUFF. A pleated cuff usually matching the neck ruff.

RUG. A rough woollen material.

RUSSET. A coarse homespun fabric.

SABLE. A fur. See page 23.

SAFEGUARD. A protective outerskirt to wear particularly on horseback.

" . . . a kind of aray or attire reaching from the navill downe to the feete, by this description like a woman's safeguard, or a baker's." (Higins, *Nomenclator*, 1585.)

In the wardrobe accounts of Queen Elizabeth the safeguard is minutely described in workmanship and material, but the form is omitted. They seem to have been accompanied by cloaks or " juppes."

SAILOR'S ATTIRE. No definite habit seems to have been worn by the sailor. Vecellio describes the English sailor as wearing a loose flaring short coat, large full breeches to the knee, an unstarched pleated ruff, and a high brimless fur hat. (*Abiti.*)

See illus. on page 35.

" The sea-mann has his cap, par'd without brim." (Dekker, *The Honest whore*, 1604.)

SANDAL. (1) A shoe with strap over the foot.

(2) Cotgrave calls : " souliers à bride—sandals ; or wooden pattens held unto the foot by one, or more strings which fastened on both sides of their sole, thence runne, and rayne, over the instep."

(3) Covering for the foot, put on by Bishop vesting for Mass, after Buskins.

SARCENET. A thin silk fabric.

" A light veil of sarsnet. (Tomkis, *Lingua*, 1607.)

" A (corporal's) scarf of red and white sarsnet." (Davies, *England's Trainings*, 1619.)

SATIN. This fabric was extensively used at this period.

SAY. A cloth of fine texture resembling serge ; in the 16th century sometimes partly of silk.

SCABBARD. Sheath of sword, rapier, dagger or knife.

" The English and French have one peculiar fashion, which I never observed in any other part, namely to weare scabbards and sheaths of velvet upon their rapiers and daggers." (Moryson's *Itinerary*.)

SCALINGS. See SCAVILONES.

SCAPULARI. A chasuble-like garment with hood worn by Benedictine, Dominican and Carthusian monks. See MONASTIC ORDERS.

SCARF. " . . . they must have their silk scarffes cast about their faces, and fluttering in the winde, with great tassels at every end, either of gold, silver or silk." (Stubbes, *Anatomy of Abuses.*)

" Why in the Stop-throate fashion doth he go, With Scarfe about his necke ? " (S. Rowlands' *Epigram*, 27.)

As a military officer's sash see BALDRICK.

" . . . under your arm like a lieutenant's scarf." (Shakespeare, *Much Ado About Nothing*—II. I. 200.)

Also, a broad black band of silk worn like a stole, around back of neck and hanging down each side. Worn by doctors of divinity, and clerical authorities of collegiate and cathedral bodies." (Macalister, *Ecclesiastical Vestments.*)

See STOLE, TIPPET.

SCAVILONES or SCALINGS. " In English we meet with scalings, scabilonians, scavilones, as apparent synonyms of canions." (F. M. Kelly.)

(In preparation for combat) " Nayler put off hys nether stockes, and so bare foote and bare legged save hys silke scavilones to the anckles . . .came in." (Holinshed, 1577.)

" Great britches, gascogne hose, scalings, nor any other like monstrous and unseemly apparell." (Ecclesiastical Proclamation of Bishop Barnes, 1577.)

SCEPTRE. See illus. on page 84.

SCIMITAR. A short curved single edge sword used largely by Orientals. It is mentioned by Cervantes (*Don Quixote*) in reference to weapons of the Moors.

SENDAL. " ' Sendale ' . . . was a thynne stuffe lyke sarcenette . . . but courser and narrower than the Sarcenett nowe ys." (Thynne, 1599.)

SERJEANT-AT-LAW. See page 82.

SERVANT'S WEAR. See LIVERY.

SETTING STICKS. " They also have another instrument called a setting sticke either of wood or bone, and sometimes of gold and silver, made forked wise at both ends, and with this they set their ruffes." (Stubbes, *Anatomy of Abuses.*)

SHAG. A sort of stuff like plush. (Planché.)

SHEATH. See SCABBARD.

SHIELD. " His shield of hard leather was borne after him." (Holinshed, 1571, as quoted by Nichols.)

" But in a day of battaile the old Roman shield, and a short sharp-pointed sword, to execute in a throng of men, exceedes the Halberd and browne-bill." (E. Davies, *England's Trainings*, 1619.)

See TARGET, RONDACHE, BUCKLER.

SHIFT. See SMOCK.

SHIRT. Innermost garment worn by men.

" Item—ix shertes whereof iiii whyte sherts, ii blacke, a blewe one edged wth gold and one wth silver—40 shilling." Folger Manuscript. (*Inventorye of the goods . . . of George Cope*, 1572).

" . . . being in his shirt, as if he meant to play at tennis." (John Taylor's *Travailes*, 1621.)

" Their Shirtes, which all in a manner doe weare . . . are eyther of Camericke, Holland, Lawne, or els of the finest cloth that may bee got . . . wrought through out with nedle work of silke, and suche like, and curiouslie stitched with open seame, and many other knackes besydes . . ." (Stubbes, *Anatomy of Abuses.*)

SHOE. Shoes in great variety may be studied throughout the illustrations. They were made of stout or of light leather, of velvet in various colours, or of satin. They might slip on or be tied with lacings, fastened with ribbons or shoe roses or rosettes, etc. Shoes might be straight to the ankles or with a turn-down cuff. They were usually flat heeled, or with a cork sole widening to the heel. Toward 1600 heels began to appear.

Boy : " Will you weare your single-soled shooes to-day ? "

John : " No, no, I will weare my shooes of double and three soles." (*Ortho-Epia*, John Eliot, 1593.)

" Foot gear " may be studied under the following heads :

BOOTS, BOOT HOSE, CHOPINE, CLOGS, CORKED SHOES, MOYLES, PANTOFLES, PATTENS, PINSONS, PUMPS, SANDALS, SLIPPERS, STARTUPS.

SHOE STRINGS. " Tye your shooe-stringes." (Erondell's *French Garden*, 1605.)

" (He) my shooe-string craves,
And that he putteth through his eare."
(S. Rowlands' *Doctor Merrie-man*, 1607.)

See EAR STRING.

SILK. Silk was in common use for garments of all kinds.

SKIMSKIN. See MUFF.

SLEEVE. Sleeves could as a rule be detached from their foundation and affixed to others by means of points, aglets, buttons, or even pins.

The illustrations afford profuse examples of almost every form of sleeve.

SLIPPER. See PANTALOON. See illus. on page 28. See GOWN.

SLOPS. Wide loose breeches.

" Sometimes I have seene Tarleton play the clowne, and use no other breeches than such sloppes or slivings as now many gentlemen weare ; they are almost capable of a bushel of wheate, and if they be of sackcloth, they would serve to carry mawlt to the mill. This absurd, clownish, and unseemly attire only by custome now is not misliked, but rather approved." (Thomas Wright's *Passions of the minde*, 1601.)

SMOCK. Innermost garment for women, serving the purpose of a chemise or even a night-gown.

" for she'll be up twenty times a night, and there will she sit in her smock till she have writ a sheet of paper." (Shakespeare, *Much Ado About Nothing*—II. III. 146.)

" Smocke . . . of the strongest canvas." (Innkeeper's daughter in night attire.) (Cervantes' *Don Quixote*, tr. Shelton, 1612.)

Smocks are frequently mentioned among the New Year's gifts of Queen Elizabeth. From Philip Sidney she received " a smock of camerick, the sleves and collor wrought with blac worke, and edged with a small bone lace of golde and silver." (Nichols' *Progresses*.)

SNAP-HAUNCE. The earliest form of the flint-lock. This form of gun lock superseded the match-lock and the wheel-lock.

SNUFTKIN. See MUFF.

SOCK. " Socke, or linnen hose." (Baret, 1580.)

SOLDIER'S ATTIRE. There was at this period no fixed military uniform. Armour piece by piece was gradually falling into disuse. (See ARMOUR.) It will be seen by a study of the illustrations and their text how the military attire followed the general trend of civilian fashion. The arms and armour and all parts of military equipment are treated under their separate headings. See particularly, for the various branches of the service : ARCHER, BILLMAN, HALBARDIER, HARQUEBUSIER.

SPANGLES. These were used as decoration to women's gowns, petticoats, veils, gloves, hair attire, ruffs, garters.

SPECTACLES. " Her eyes which were hid with a great payre of spectacles." (Cervantes' *Don Quixote*, tr. Shelton, 1612.)

" His specktacles do in a copper case,
Hang dangling . . ." (S. Rowlands' *Satyres*, 1600.)

See illus. page 88.

SPLINTS. Armour composed of narrow strips, or horizontal overlapping plates. See ALMAIN RIVET, ANIMA.

SPURS. " . . . He walked the chamber with such a pestilent gingle that his spurs oversqueaked the lawyer, and made him reach his voice three notes above his fee ; but after we had spied the rowels of his spurs, how we blesst ourselves ! they did so much and so far exceed

the compass of our fashion, that they looked more like the forerunners of wheelbarrows." (Thomas Middleton's *The Ant and the Nightingale, or Father Hubburd's tales*, 1604.)

STAFF OF OFFICE. " The mode of appointing an important household office was by delivery of a white staff which became symbol of office and which at the funeral of the sovereign he solemnly broke over his head before the bier." (Nichols, *Progresses of Queen Elizabeth*.)

" Gentlemen ushers with white roddes." (Funeral of Queen Elizabeth, Nichols' *Progresses*.)

See CHAIN. See CROSIER.

STAMMEL—STAMEL. A kind of fine worsted (Hal). Red seems to have been its usual colour, or a certain shade of red was called stammel.

" In petticoats of stammel red." (*History of Whitcombe*, Planché.)

" Item, one cope of red stamill." (Inventory, 1552.)

STARCH. " In the yeere 1564 Mistris Dinghen van den plasse . . . came to London . . . and there professed herselfe a starcher wherein she excelled . . . Some very few of the best and most curious wives of that time . . . made them cambrick Ruffes and sent them to Mist. Dinghen to starch, and after a while they made them ruffes of Lawne which was at that time, a stuffe most strange and wonderfull . . . and then they began to send their Daughters and nearest kinsewomenne to Mist. Dinghen to Learne how to starch, her usuall price was at that time, foure or five pound to teach them how to starch . . ." (Stow's *Annales*.) See RUFF.

STATUTE CAP. See CAP.

STARTUP. " A high shooe of rawe leather called a stertup." (Baret, 1573.)

" A payre of startups had he on his feete.
That lased were up to the small of the legge :
Homelie they were, and easier than meete,
And in their soles full many a wooden peg.
(Thynne, *Debate between pride and lowliness*, 1568-70.)

" The streetes are so mirie, that you cannot walk in them without startups." (Pory, *Leo's Africa*, 1600.)

STOCKINGS. These were first made of fabric, and later they were knit. They were usually gartered above or below the knee and for men could be pulled up over the breeches or tucked under. They were of almost any colour.

See HOSE.

" Queen Elizabeth in 1561 was presented with a pair of black silk knit stockings by her silk-woman Mrs. Montague, and thenceforth she never wore cloth hose any more." (Howel, *History of the World*.)

" In the yeere 1599 was devised and perfected the art of knitting or weaving silke stockings . . . by engines or steele Loomes . . ." (Stow's *Annales*.)

" Long stockings without garters, then was the Earl of Leicester's fashion, and theirs who had the handsomest leg." (Peacham's *The truth of our times*, 1637.)

See page 31.

See BUSKINS.

STOLE. Ecclesiastical vestment consisting of a narrow band of silk or linen, nine to ten feet long, and two to three inches wide, often embroidered. It was worn over the alb or surplice and when under the chasuble it showed only its ends which were sometimes fringed.

The stole was used :

By priests, who wore it crossed on the breast.

By deacons, who wore it over the left shoulder across the back and breast to the right side.

By Bishops, who wore it around the shoulders and pendant to the knees or longer.

See TIPPET. See SCARF. See illus. on page 86.

STOMACHER. A covering for the chest and stomach, either for warmth or for ornamentation.

" The furryers doe use their skynnes for stomackgers to guard and defend the brest against the force of servent colde." (Turberville, *Falconrie*, 1575.)

" 4 stomachers of velvett trymmed with a passemayn of Venis gold on the toppes." (Nichols' *Progresses*, under gifts to Queen Elizabeth.)

See illus. on page 59.

STONE-BOW.   See Cross-bow.

STROSSERS.   Breeches.

" His Squire apparell'd in a yellow Coat, with wide sleeves, and strossers cut in paines of yellow and watchet." (Jones and Davenant, *Brit. Trium.*, 1637.)

" . . . sets his son a horse-backe in cloth-of-gold breeches while he himself goes to the devil a-foot in a pair of old strossers." (Middleton's *No wit like a woman's*, 1613.)

" And you rode, like a kern of Ireland, your French hose off and in your straight strossers." (Shakespeare, *Henry V*—III. VII. 60.)

SUPPORTASSE.   " . . . A certain device made of wyers, crested for the purpose, whipped over either with gold, thred, silver or silk, and this hee calleth a supportasse, or underpropper.   This is to be applyed round about their necks under the ruffe, upon the outside of the band, to bear up the whole frame and body of the ruffe from falling and hanging down." (Stubbes, *Anatomy of Abuses*.)

SURPLICE.   Liturgical vestment worn by both Catholic and Protestant clergy.   It was a tunic of white linen or cotton with wide pendent sleeves, and was passed over the head, having no opening at the neck.   Its length varied between knee and ankle.

The surplice was worn in place of the alb and over the fur - lined cassock when no vestment of importance (except the cope, which was adaptable) was put over it. (Macalister, *Ecclesiastical Vestments*.)

SWORD.   The sword or the rapier may be studied throughout the illustrations in this work.

It appears to have been generally worn by all men and boys with the following exceptions :

(1) " No man travelleth by the waie without his sword, or some such weapon with us ; except the Minister, who commonlie weareth none at all, unlesse it be a dagger or a hanger at his side." (Harrison.)

(2) Among the regulations of 1582, the apprentice was forbidden to carry a sword.

(3) The Fellows of the Inns of Court wore no weapons except a dagger or a knife, nor could they cause any sword to be borne after them into town.

The sword was used on ceremonial occasions as a symbol of honour or authority. (See illus. on pages 61 and 81.)

" Where's your blue coat, your sword and buckler, sir ?

Get you such like habit for a serving man."
(N. Field's *Two Angry Women*, 1599.)

TABARD.   " A jaquet or sleeveless coat worn in times past by noblemen in the warres, but now only by heraults, and is called theyr coat of armes in servyse." (Specht's *Glossary*, 1597.)

See Herald's Coat.   See page 80.

TABBINET.   A silk fabric.

TABBY.   " A kind of course silk taffety watered." (Bailey, *Dictionary*, 1721.)

TACE—TASSETS.   That part of armour which protected the front of the body from the waist to the thigh or even to the knee.   It was made of horizontal strips of steel called " lames."

See illus. on pages 93 and 94.

TACKE.   A form of pistol.

TAFFETA.   This silk fabric was extensively used at this period, though considered a luxury.

TAG.   See Aglet.

TARGET.   A round or oval shield.

See Buckler.

TASSELS.   See Pike.   See Scarf.

TAWDRY  LACE.   Cheap, showy ribbons worn by country girls.

THRUM.   Any loose thread or fringe or a tuft of filaments or fibres. (*Standard Dictionary*.)

A thrummed hat was one made of very coarse woollen cloth. (Minsheu, *Guide unto Tongues*.)

See Cap.

TIARA.   A triple crown surmounted by a cross worn by the Pope in public, on certain occasions, as a sign of his temporal power.   It was not worn at liturgical functions, at which time the mitre was worn.

See illus. on page 85.

TIFFANY.   A thin silk or gauze.

" The invention of that fine silke, Tiffanie, Sarcenet, and Cypres, which instead of apparell to cover and hide, shew women naked through them." (Holland, *Pliny*, 1601.)

TIPPET.   A scarf worn over the shoulders with ends hanging down in front, or less commonly, a cape made of fur or cloth edged or lined with fur.   It was worn by doctors of divinity, heads of colleges, members of cathedral bodies and chaplains of noblemen. (H. Druitt, *Costume on Brasses*.)

" [He] shall weare a typpet of velvett as other Aldermen have accustomyd yn thoffyce of Mayraltie to do." (Turner, *Sel. Rec. Oxford*, 1554.)

" Priestes should be otherwise knowne then by their shaven crownes and typets." (Bradford in *Coverdale Lett. Mart.*, 1555.)

" It shall be lawful for such ministers as are not graduates to wear upon their surplices instead of hoods, some decent tippet of black, so it be not silk." (*Cons. and Canons Eccles.*, 1604.)

See Judge's Attire.

" For you shall not see as much as one Venetian there of the Patrician ranke without his black gowne and tippet." (Coryat's *Crudities*, 1611.)

TOBACCO BOX.   " Our gallant must draw out his Tobacco-box, the ladell for the cold snuffe, into the nosthrill, the tongs and prining-Iron : all which artillery may be of gold or silver (if he can reach the price of it). "

See Pipe.

TONSURE.   The shaven crown of a priest's head.

TOOTHPICK.   " Item, six smale tothe-picks of golde. Geven by Mrs. Snowe, one of them lost by her Majestie." (New Year's gift to Queen Elizabeth, 1574, Nichols' *Progresses of Queen Elizabeth*.)

" Make thee a tooth-picke of a litle quill or of a litle peece of wood with a sharpe pointe." (Hollybande, *The French Schoolmaster*, 1573.)

TOUCH-BOX.   A receptacle for gunpowder, similar to the powder flask but smaller.

See Harquebusier.

TOURNAMENT.   See illus. on page 92.

See *History of the Tournament*, by Cripps-Day, with its full bibliography.

TRAIN (of a gown).   See pages 9 and 14.

TROWSE, TROWSER, TROSSER.   (See also Strosser.) In Ben Jonson's *The Staple of News*, Pennyboy, Jr., " walks up and down in his gown, waistcoat and trowses, expecting his tailor," and when the tailor arrives he says, " . . . leaving me to stalk here in my trowses ? " Would this seem that the " trowses " were an undergarment ?  See Undergarments.

TRUNK HOSE.   Short, full breeches.

See Breeches.

TRUNK SLEEVES.   Wide sleeves bolstered out by wire or padding.   See page 39.

TUCKE.   " Espée Espagnole, a Rapier or Tucke." (Cotgrave, 1611.)

TUFT-TAFFETA.   A taffeta with some sort of pile, or nap which apparently resembled worn velvet :

" Sleeveless his jerkin was, and it had been
Velvet, but t'was now (so much ground was seen)
Become Tufftaffety ; and our children shall
See it plain rash a while, then nought at all."
(Donne's *Satires*, 1593-4.)

" Item, one loose gowne of black tufte Taphata." (Folger manuscript.   Wardrobe accounts of Queen Elizabeth, 1600.) See Velvet.

TUNICLE. A less ample variety of the dalmatic used by sub-deacons at Mass. Bishops wore it below the dalmatic.

See illus. on page 86.

UMBRELLA. "An umbrello of perfumed leather with a gould fryndge abowte yt which I broughte out of Italie." (Will of R. Toft, 1618, Fairholt.)

See page 20.

UNDERGARMENTS. The shirt for men and the smock for women were the usual inner garments of the time. The women wore over the smock a sort of corset which was called " privie coat " or " petty-coate bodyes " or " whale bone bodies," and the farthingale, also the petticoat or the kirtle or both. Men wore upon the shirt, the doublet which was usually covered by the jerkin. Both sexes wore at times a waistcoat for warmth or for decoration, which could be concealed or not.

See the above articles under their various headings.

" Two paire of linnen breeches next the skin, three paire of linnen hose under the stockings." (Minsheu, *Pleasant and delightful dialogues*, 1623.)

See Moryson's amusing allusions, page 15.

See also allusion under TROWSE.

UPPER STOCKS. See BREECHES. See HOSE.

VAMBRACE. Armour for the arm. See page 94.

" And in my vantbrace put this wither'd brawn." (Shakespeare, *Troilus*—I. III. 297.)

VAMPLATE. An iron disk on the tilting lance to protect the hand.

VANDELAS. A kind of canvas.

VARDINGALE. See FARTHINGALE.

VASQUINE. See BASQUINE.

VEIL. See its use on page 57.

VELA. See NUN'S ATTIRE.

VELVET. Extensively used at this time and often mentioned throughout this work.

VENETIANS. Breeches terminating below the knees.

See BREECHES.

VENICE GOLD. Gold thread manufactured in Venice. Venice silver was also used.

" Valance of Venice gold in needle-work." (Shakespeare, *Taming of the Shrew*—II. I. 348.)

See LACE.

VENTAILLE. See BEAVER.

VESTES. A gown worn by monks or nuns.

See NUNS. See MONASTIC ORDERS.

VESTMENT. (The chasuble was sometimes called " vestment.") Ecclesiastical vestments have varied but little in the past few hundred years. The advent of of Protestantism naturally brought great changes, or rather simplifications in the vesture of the clergy. These, as well as the vestments of the Roman church are treated under their individual headings.

See illus. on pages 85, 86 and 87.

Following is a Tabulation showing what colours were worn in certain articles of Ecclesiastical Attire upon specific occasions :

### WHITE

| | |
|---|---|
| Christmas Day | Corpus Christi |
| St. John the Evangelist | Feasts of the Virgin Mary |
| Epiphany | St. John Baptist |
| Circumcision | St. Michael |
| Candlemas | All Saints |
| Easter | Confessors |
| Ascension | Virgins |
| Dedication of a church. | Transfiguration. |
| Harvest Festival. | Confirmation. |
| Trinity Sunday | |

### RED.

| | |
|---|---|
| St. Stephen. | Martyrs. |
| Holy Innocents (if a Sunday). | Apostles. |
| | Evangelists. |
| Pentecost. | Holy Cross. |

### VIOLET.

| | |
|---|---|
| Advent to Christmas Eve. | Septuagesima to Maunday |
| Holy Innocents. | Thursday. |
| Procession of candles before mass. | Rogation Days. |

### ROSE.

Christmas Eve (if a Sunday).

### BLACK.

| | |
|---|---|
| Advent to Christmas Eve. | Good Friday. |
| Requiem. | |

(From *Ecclesiastical Vestments*, Macalister.)

See PRIEST'S VESTMENTS.

VEXILLUM. Scarf which was tied about the crozier, also called INFULA. See illus. on page 86.

VISOR. The face guard of a steel helmet. The visor was strictly the upper part, pierced for sight, while the beaver was the lower section. These parts could move up and down on a pivot placed above the ear.

See BEAVER. See illus. on page 94.

VIZARD—VISOR. See MASK.

" For they must all be mask'd and vizarded." (Shakespeare, *Merry Wives*—IV. VI. 40.)

WAISTCOAT. A garment worn by both men and women, and serving various purposes.

" Why have you taken your wast-coates ? Is it so colde ? " (Erondell's *French Garden*, 1605.)

" So opening and putting off his doublet, he was in a Scarlet Wastecoate." (Execution of the Earl of Essex, Stow's *Annales*.)

" Enter A . . . and P . . . in their wast-cotes with rackets." (B. Barnes, *Devils Charter*, 1607.)

" . . . his wast-coat (which showed itself under the unbuttoned doublet) not unlike the best sort of those woollen knit ones, which our ordinary watermen row us in." (*Life of Sidney*, by Fulke Greville, in reference to the attire of the Prince of Orange.)

Waistcoats are frequently mentioned among the New Year's gifts of Queen Elizabeth : " A wastecoate of white taffety, imbrodered all over with a twist of flowers of Venis gold, silver, and some black silke." (Nichols' *Progresses of Queen Elizabeth*.)

They were also made of lawn, of sarcenet or even of flannel ; though their form is not mentioned, they were probably akin to the doublet.

WATCH. Under " jewelles geven to her Majestie at Newyers-tyde," appear several watches and little clocks set in gold, in mother of pearl, garnished with jewels and pendants. (Nichols' *Progresses*.)

Malvolio : " I frown the while ; and perchance wind up my watch." (Shakespeare, *Twelfth Night*—II. V. 66.)

WATCHET. Pale blue colour.

WEDDING ATTIRE. " The bride came into the chapell with a coronet of pearle on her head, and her haire disheveled, and hanging down over her shoulders." (Peacham, describing the marriage of Princess Elizabeth with the Palsgrave.)

" Bridegroom . . . with a paire of greene Garters tyed cross above the knee, and a doozen of Crewell Points that set out his hose verie faire. Thus with a branche of Rosemarie marched Tomkins to the church where Kate he met, and there, to be breefe, they were married." (R. Greene, *Greene's Vision*, 1592.)

" . . . she was lead to church between two sweet boys with bride-laces and rosemary tied about their silken sleeves . . . Then was there a fair bride-cup of silver and gilt carried before her, wherein was a goodly branch of rosemary, gilded very fair, hung about with silken ribands of all colours . . . " (Thomas Deloney.)

" . . . and though your ladyship did not honour his nuptials with your presence, he hath by me sent each of you a pair of gloves . . ." (Nathaniel Field, *Amends for Ladies*, 1618.)

See BRIDE LACE. See HAIR. See GLOVE.

AMMAN, Jost—*Habitus Præcipuorum*, 1577.

BAILEY, Nathaniel—*Universal Etymological English Dictionary*, 1721.

BARET, John—*Dictionarie*, 1573-80.

BARRET, Robert—*The theorike and practike of moderne warres*, 1597-8.

BARTLETT, John—*Concordance to Shakespeare*, 1894.

BEAUMONT, Francis, and John FLETCHER—*Cupids revenge*, 1615.

BECK, S. W.—*Drapers Dictionary*, 1886.

*†BOEHN, Max von—*Modes and Manners*, Vol. II. 1932-3.

BONANNI, Filippo—*Catalogo degli ordini religiosi Della Chiesa Militante*, 1707.

BRANTOME, Pierre de Bourdeilles de—*Mémoires*. (Died 1614.) Ed. Lalanne, 1896.

BRAUN, Joseph—*Die Liturgische Gewandung*, 1907.

*BRUYN, Abraham De—*Costumes Civils & Militaires*, 1872. A facsimile reprint of *Habitus Variarum Gentium*, 1581.

BRY, De, Theodorus (Dirk) and Johannes—*Collectiones Peregrinationum in Indiam Orientalem et Indiam Occidentalem*, 1590-1634.

BURKE'S PEERAGE.

*†*BURLINGTON MAGAZINE*—Articles by F. M. Kelly, March, June, 1914; June, Sept., Dec., 1916.

CAMDEN, William—*Annales*, 1615.

CARDWELL, Edward—*Synodalia, a Collection of Articles of Religion, Canons, and Proceedings of Convocation from 1547-1717*. 1842.

*CATHOLIC ENCYCLOPEDIA*, 1907.

CERVANTES, Miguel de—*Don Quixote*, 1604. First English trans. by T. Shelton, 1612.

CLAYTON, Henry James—*The Ornaments of the Ministers as shown on English Monumental Brasses*, 1919. (Alcuin Club collections.)

CLEPHAN, R. C.—*The Tournament*, 1919.

COOKE, Richard—*La Première Partie du Compte de Richarde Cooke de Kent pour son Voiage et temps employé en France*, 1584.

†CORYAT, Thomas—*Coryats Crudities*, 1611.

COTGRAVE, Randle—*A Dictionarie of the French and English tongues* 1611 and 1632.

CRIPPS-DAY, F. H.—*History of the Tournament*, 1918.

CROWLEY, Robert—*One and thyrtye epigrammes*, 1550.

CUNNINGHAM, P.—*Account of Court Revels*. (Ed. 1842.)

CUST, Sir Lionel Henry—*Historical and descriptive catalogue of the pictures, busts, etc., in the National Portrait Gallery*, 1896.

DAVIES, Edward—*The Art of War and England's Traynings*, 1619.

DEKKER, Thomas—*Guls horne-booke*, 1609; *Patient Grissill*, 1603; *The honest whore*, 1604; *Seven deadly sins of London*, 1606.

DILLON, H. A.—*Archæological Journal*. Vol. LXI and LV. (See Fairholt.)

DONNE, John—*Satires*, 1593-7.

DRUITT, Herbert—*Costume on Brasses*, 1906.

*†DUCHARTRE, Pierre L.—*The Italian Comedy*. Eng. Trans. 1929.

DU CANGE, Charles Du Fresne—*Glossarium* (Ed. 1840-50).

DUGDALE, Sir W.—*Origines Juridiciales*, 1666 and 1671.

D'URFEY, Thomas—*Wit and Mirth, or pills to purge melancholy*.

ELIOT, John—*Ortho-epia gallica*, 1593. Ed. by Jack Lindsay, 1928.

*ELIZABETHAN ART*. Burlington Fine Arts Club, 1926.

ELYOT, Sir Thomas—*Dictionary*, 1538.

*ENCYCLOPÆDIA BRITANNICA*, 14th Edition

†ERONDELL, Peter—*The French Garden*, 1605. (Haslewood Reprint, 1925.)

EVELYN, John—*Diary*, 1641-1705.

FAIRHOLT, F. W.—*Costume in England*. Edited by Lord Dillon, 1896.

FAVYN, André—*Theatre of Honour*, 1623.

*†FFOULKES, C. S.—*The Armourer and his Craft*, 1912.

FIELD, Nathaniel—*A woman is a weathercocke*, 1612; *Amends for ladies*, 1618; *Two Angry Women*, 1599.

FITZGEFFREY, Henry—*Satyres and Satyricall Epigrams*, 1617; *Certain Elegies done by sundrie excellent wits*, 1618.

FLETCHER, John—See BEAUMONT.

FLORIO, John—*A Worlde of Wordes*, 1598; *Second Fruits*, 1591; *Translation Montaigne's Essayes*, 1603.

*FOSSARD—*Recueil Fossard*. Recueil de plusieurs fragments des premières Comédies Italiennes qui ont été représentées en France sous le règne de Henri III. Conservé au Musée National de Stockholm. Ed. Duchartre Paris, 1928.

*FRANCO, G.—*Habiti delle donne Venetiane; Habiti d'Huomeni e Donne Venetiane*; Reprint of the edition of 1610, with French, German and English text, 1876.

GASCOIGNE, George—*The Storie of Ferdinando Jeronimo* in *Works*, 1587.

GAY, Victor—*Glossaire archéologique du moyen age et de la renaissance*, 1882-1928.

GHEYN, Jacob de—*Maniement d'armes, d'arquebuses, mousquets et piques*, 1608.

GOSSON, Stephen—*Pleasant quippes for upstart new-fangled gentlewomen*, 1595.

GREENE, Robert—*Never too late*, 1590; *Greenes vision*, 1592; *A quip for an upstart courtier*, 1592.

GREVILLE, Fulke—*The life of the renowned Sir Philip Sidney*, Pub. 1652.

HALL, Joseph—*Satires*, 1597-8.

HALLIWELL, James O.—*Dictionary of Archaic and Provincial Words*, 1904.

HARINGTON, Sir John—*Nugæ Antiquæ* (1792 Ed.).

†HARRISON'S *Description of England in Shakspere's Youth*. Edited from the first two editions of Holinshed's Chronicle, 1577-87. Edited by F. J. Furnivall, 1877.

HAWKINS, Sir Richard—*Observations in his voiage into the South Sea*, 1593 (Pubd. 1622).

HENSLOWE, Philip—*Henslowe's Diary*, 1592-1609. Ed. W. W. Greg, 1904-8.

HEYLYN, Peter—*Ecclesia Restaurata; History of the Reformation of the Church of England*, 1661.

HEYWOOD, Thomas—*Rape of Lucrece*, 1608.

*HIERURGIA ANGLICANA*. Edited by Vernon Staley, 1902-3.

HIGINS—*Junius' Nomenclator*, 1585.

*HIRTH, Georg—*Kulturgeschichtliches Bilderbuch*, 1881-90. Vols. II-III.

HOLINSHED, Raphael—*The Chronicles of England, Scotlande and Irelande*, 1577-8.

†HOLLYBAND, Claudius—*The French Schoolmaster*, 1573; *A Dictionary French and English*, 1593; *Treasurie of the French tong*, 1580.

HOLME, Randal—*Academy of Armory*, 1688.

HUTTON, Henry—*Follie's Anatomie*, 1619.

*†JONES, Inigo—*Designs for Masques and Plays at Court*. (Walpole Soc., Pub.) See WALPOLE.

JONSON, Benjamin—*Every man in his Humour*, 1601 ; *Every man out of his Humour*, 1600 ; *Cynthia's revels*, 1601 ; *The Devil is an ass*, 1616 ; *The staple of news*, 1625.

KELLIE, Thomas—*Militarie instructions*, printed 1627.

*†KELLY, F. M. and R. SCHWABE—*Historic Costume*, 1925 ; *A Short History of Costume and Armour*, 1931.

†KLARWILL, Victor von—*Queen Elizabeth and Some Foreigners*. Being a series of hitherto unpublished letters from the archives of the Hapsburg family, 1928.

*†LAKING, G. F.—*Record of European Armour*. 1920-22.

LANT, Thomas—*Funeral of Sir Philip Sidney*, 1587.

LATIMER, Hugh—*Remains* and *Sermons*, 1552.

LODGE, Thomas—*Wits Miserie*, 1596.

LYLY, John—*Midas*, 1592.

MACALISTER, R. A. S.—*Ecclesiastical Vestments*, 1896.

MAISSE, De—*A Journal of all that was Accomplished by Monsieur De Maisse, Ambassador in England from King Henri IV to Queen Elizabeth*, 1597. Trans. by G. B. Harrison and R. A. Jones, 1931.

MARKHAM, Gervase—*The souldier's accidence*, 1625.

MARSTON, John—*Antonio and Mellida*, 1601 ; *Dutch Courtezan*, 1605 ; *Jack Drum's entertainment*, 1601 ; *Malcontent*, 1604 ; *The scourge of villainie (three books of satyres)*, 1598.

MASSINGER, Philip—*A new way to pay old debts*, 1632-3 ; *The Fatall Dowry*, 1632.

MEYRICK, S. R.—*A Critical Inquiry into Antient Armour*, 1824.

MIDDLETON, Thomas—*Father Hubbard's tales, or the ant and the nightingale*, 1604 ; *Blacke booke*, 1604 ; *The triumphs of love and antiquity*, 1619 ; *No wit no help like a woman's*, 1613.

MINSHEU, J.—*The guide unto tongues*, 1617 ; *Pleasant and delightfull dialogues in Spanish and English*, 1623.

MONTAIGNE, Michel de—*The essayes*, 1580-1592. Florio Trans. 1603.

*MOREAU-NELATON, E.—*Les Clouets et Leurs Emules*, 1924.

†MORYSON, Fynes—*Itinerary*. Published 1617 (Written 1605-17).

NASHE, Thomas—*Pierce Penilesse, his supplication to the divell*, 1592 ; *Christ's tears over Jerusalem*, 1593.

†NICHOLS, John—*Progresses of Queen Elizabeth*, 1788 and 1823 ; *Progresses of James I*, 1828.

NICOLAS, N. H.—*Testamenta Vestusta*, 1826.

*†NICOLL, Allardyce—*Masks Mimes and Miracles*, 1931.

ONIONS, C. T.—*A Shakespeare Glossary*, 1929.

*OXFORD DICTIONARY*. Ed. J. A. H. Murray, 1888-1926.

PALLISER, Mrs. Bury—*History of Lace*. Ed. Jourdain and Dryden, 1902.

PEACHAM, Henry—*The truth of our times*, 1637.

PEELE, George—*The old wives tale*, 1595.

PLANCHE, J. R.—*Cyclopædia of Costume*, 1878.

*PLUVINEL, Antoine de—*L'instruction Du Roy en l'exercice de monter à cheval*, 1623. (Probably written several years earlier.)

POLLARD, A. W., and G. R. REDGRAVE—*A Short-Title Catalogue of Books Printed in England, Scotland and Ireland and of English Books Printed Abroad*, 1447-1640. 1926.

PORTER, Henry—*The pleasant history of two angry women of Abington*, 1599.

PUGIN, A. W.—*Glossary of Ecclesiastical Ornament and Costume*, 1868.

QUICHERAT, J.—*Histoire du Costume en France*, 1875.

RANDOLPH—*Hey for Honesty*, 1651.

RICH, Barnabie—*Opinion defied*, 1613 ; *A Pathway to military practise*, 1587.

ROBINSON, Rev. N. F.—*St. Paul's Ecc. Society Publication*, Vol. IV.

ROCK, Rev. Daniel—*Church of our Fathers*, 1849-54.

ROWLANDS, Samuel—*Doctor Merry-man his medicines*, 1607 ; *The knave of harts—Haile fellow well met*, 1612 ; *A pair of spy-knaves*, 1619 ; *Humors looking glasse*, 1608 ; *The Letting of Humour's Blood*, 1600.

*ROXBURGHE BALLADS*.

RYE, W. B.—*England as Seen by Foreigners*, 1865.

SEGAR, William—*Honor, military and civill*, 1602.

SELDEN, John—*Titles of honor*, 1614.

SHAKESPEARE, William—*All's Well that Ends Well* ; *Hamlet* ; 1st Part of *Henry IV* ; 2nd part *Henry IV* ; *Henry V* ; 2nd part of *Henry VI* ; *Henry VIII* ; *Richard II* ; *Richard III* ; *Pericles* ; *Taming of the Shrew* ; *Troilus and Cressida* ; *Twelfth Night* ; *As You Like It* ; *Macbeth* ; *Two Gentlemen of Verona* ; *Merry Wives of Windsor* ; *Tempest* ; *Much Ado About Nothing* ; *Winter's Tale*.

*†*SHAKESPEARE'S ENGLAND*—Oxford University Press, 1917.

SMITH, John—*General Historie of Virginia, New England and the Summer Isles*, 1624.

SMYTHE, Sir John—*Certain Discourses, concerning divers sorts of weapons*, 1590.

SPENSER, Edmund—*Faerie Queene*, 1589-90.

STOW, John—*Annales*, 1580-1605, continued by E. Howes to 1631 ; *Survey of London*, 1598 ; *Chronicles*, 1580.

STRICKLAND, Agnes—*Letters of Mary Queen of Scots*, 1864.

†STUBBES, Philip—*The Anatomy of Abuses*. 1583-5-95. Edited by F. J. Furnival, 1877-9-82.

STYWARD, Thomas—*The pathwaie to martiall discipline*, 1581.

TAYLOR, John—*Superbiæ flagellum or The whip of pride*, 1621 ; *Travailes*, 1621 ; *The Young Gallant's Whirligig*, 1629.

THYNNE, Francis—*The debate between pride and lowliness*, 1570.

TOMKIS, Thomas—*Lingua, or the combat of the tongue*, 1607.

TOPF, Jacob—*An almain armourers album*. Ed. Dillon, 1905.

TURBERVILLE, George—*The booke of faulconrie or hauking*, 1575.

VECELLIO, Cesare—*Degli Abiti Antichi e Moderni*, 1590. (Reprint by Firmen Didot.)

VILLAMONT, J. de—*Voyages du Seigneur de Villamont*, 1595. (Pub. 1607.)

*WALPOLE SOCIETY—*Third Annual Volume (Portraits by Gheeraerts)* ; °†*Twelfth Annual Volume (Masques)* ; °†*Fourth Annual Volume (Elizabeth's Visit to Blackfriars)*.

WILLIAMS, Sir Roger—*A briefe discourse of warre*, 1590.

WILLSON, D. H.—*Parliamentary Diary of Robert Bowyer*, 1606-7.

WRIGHT, Thomas—*The passions of the minde*, 1601.

\* *Especially recommended for its illustrations.*

† *Especially recommended for its text.*

# INDEX TO THE ILLUSTRATIONS

*Capital letters indicate acknowledged portraits.*